# MAO TSE-TUNG

# OTHER BOOKS BY JULES ARCHER

AFRICAN FIREBRAND: KENYATTA OF KENYA

ANGRY ABOLITIONIST: WILLIAM LLOYD GARRISON

BATTLEFIELD PRESIDENT: DWIGHT D. EISENHOWER

COLOSSUS OF EUROPE: METTERNICH

CONGO

THE DICTATORS

THE EXECUTIVE "SUCCESS"

THE EXTREMISTS: GADFLIES OF AMERICAN SOCIETY

FIGHTING JOURNALIST: HORACE GREELEY

FRONT-LINE GENERAL: DOUGLAS MACARTHUR

HAWKS, DOVES AND THE EAGLE

HO CHI MINH: LEGEND OF HANOI

INDIAN FOE, INDIAN FRIEND

LAWS THAT CHANGED AMERICA

MAN OF STEEL: JOSEPH STALIN

1968: YEAR OF CRISIS

PHILIPPINES' FIGHT FOR FREEDOM

RED REBEL: TITO OF YUGOSLAVIA

REVOLUTION IN OUR TIME

SCIENCE EXPLORER: ROY CHAPMAN ANDREWS

THORN IN OUR FLESH: CASTRO'S CUBA

TREASON IN AMERICA: DISLOYALTY VERSUS DISSENT

TWENTIETH CENTURY CAESAR: BENITO MUSSOLINI

THE UNPOPULAR ONES

WORLD CITIZEN: WOODROW WILSON

# MAO TSE - TUNG

by Jules Archer

HAWTHORN BOOKS, INC.

Publishers • New York

MAO TSE-TUNG

Designed by Ellen E. Gal

2 3 4 5 6 7 8 9 10

To Australia
for giving me a wife, three sons, a
daughter by marriage, and last but
not least, magnificent friends like
Russ and Eve Clark

# Contents

# Introduction

One of the oldest civilized countries in the world, China has a recorded history of almost four thousand years. Every fourth person on earth is Chinese, and they occupy a massive land area one-third larger than the United States.

"The world's peace rests with China," United States Secretary of State John Hay said in the early 1900's, "and whoever understands China socially, politically, economically, religiously, holds the key to world politics during the next five centuries." For over two decades following World War II, however, Americans were kept ignorant of China, deprived of diplomatic and press contact during a period of the greatest changes in China's long history.

News about Mao and China during the 1950's and 1960's reached Americans only indirectly from travelers coming out of China, State Department analyses of Peking's press and radio reports, interviews with foreign diplomats and journalists, and observations by veteran "China-watchers" stationed in Hong Kong. Those who tried to make sense of developments behind the "bamboo curtain" were often more baffled than enlightened.

"In Chinese philosophy," explained France's leading Sinologist, Jacques Guillermaz, "there is no such category as 'logic.' . . . The Chinese are extremely subtle, intelligent, intuitive, changeable, but often inaccessible to our reasoning."

This biography of Mao Tse-tung, reconstructed by patient literary detective work from literally hundreds of sources, Chinese and non-Chinese, is an attempt to present a clear and unbiased picture of the man, his times, his goals, his successes and failures, his virtues and frailties. Perhaps a better understanding of Mao and his China will add to an informed American public opinion, which now seems determined to permit no more tragic Asian foreign policy blunders like that of Vietnam to be made in its name.

The author is grateful to the staffs of the Mid-Hudson Library system and Adriance Library, both in Poughkeepsie, New York, for their invaluable help in assembling difficult-to-obtain material.

# MAO TSE-TUNG

# Chapter 1

# Schoolboy Rebel

Two Red Army men rode their mules past a cluster of landlords' heads dangling from a tripod in the middle of the dirt street of Ningtu in Kiangsi Province, China. On their way back from an inspection of front-line defenses both men wore simple peak caps, sweat-stained coarse tunics, puttees, and no insignia of rank. But they were each worth one hundred thousand dollars dead or alive to Generalissimo Chiang Kai-shek, leader of the Chinese Nationalists.

The taller Communist with long black hair and almond eyes set in a round flat face was forty-one-year-old Mao Tse-tung, chief of the Red Chinese. The other soldier was Chu Teh, a short, burly man of forty-five, Commander in Chief of the Chinese Red Army under Mao.

The two men turned their mules toward a low building that stood on one side of an open mud-walled courtyard. They could smell the canned soup and boiled millet cooking on the earthen stove. As they dismounted, Kuomintang planes suddenly roared low over the tin roofs of Ningtu, guns winking.

Both men flung themselves headlong against the base of one wall as the first whistle of bombs screamed through the afternoon haze. The street exploded in a maelstrom of blood, bone, and dust. Men, women, and children ran screaming in all directions.

Three dive bombers angled in from the west. A row of wooden buildings collapsed under a running salvo of high explosive. The anguished braying of panicked donkeys rose out of the billowing smoke and flame. Fighters skimmed in over the debris, raking the length of Ningtu with machine-gun fire, as though probing for the two Red leaders.

Raising his head, Mao saw the street littered with dead bodies, human and animal. A sharp smell of cordite mingled with the hot reek of blood and a burning odor of dust. He could hear the *whoom-whoom-whoom* of explosions in towns and villages to the north and northwest.

Nationalist pilots dove persistently on Ningtu across the setting sun. A stick of high explosives bracketed the tavern in cataclysmic thunder. Mao bounced into the air as great clods of earth skyrocketed. The tavern collapsed in huge columns of red dust. Smoke, belching upward amid the yellow flash of explosions, released an earthy, sour smell from the walls.

Time was clearly running out for the Communists. Daily air assaults such as this one on a beautiful autumn afternoon in October, 1934, were steadily reducing the Red bastion in Kiangsi Province to rubble. After trying to smash the Red Army for seven years, Chiang Kai-shek seemed on the verge of total victory at last.

With China plunged in the chaos of civil war Japan had attacked and seized Manchuria. But Chiang continued to see the Chinese Communists as the priority threat. Hoping to wipe out their Kiangsi stronghold in southeast China, he was convinced that smaller soviets in the north would then collapse.

This day's air raid lasted twenty minutes. When it ended, the two Red leaders rose unhurt amid the flames and smoking desolation. But both knew they could not hold out much longer. Chiang's last siege alone had cost them sixty thousand men. He had four hundred planes, and they had none.

Chiang's German military adviser, General Ludwig von Falkenhausen, had now thrown a "fire wall"—small, heavily fortified posts with scorched earth between—around the province. No supplies could get in; no refugees could get out.

Chiang had confidently predicted the fall of Kiangsi by June, 1934. Already five months behind schedule, the Kuomintang announced that their "extermination campaign" had nevertheless killed or starved a million Communists in Kiangsi.

Surrender seemed Mao's only realistic option. But he knew that if the Red Army laid down their arms, the Nationalists would slaughter them to the last man, woman, and child.

Beating the red dust from his crumpled dark-gray uniform, Mao told Chu Teh that he had reached a decision. They must do the impossible—break through the "fire wall" and the seven hundred thousand Kuomintang troops that, like a giant noose, were slowly strangling their soviet and then fight free to the north. It was a historic decision that would have earthshaking consequences, not merely for China but for the world.

According to Asian astrologers, Mao Tse-tung was born in the year of the black snake at the hour of the green dragon—a "certain" sign that he was destined for a life of incessant violence and bloodshed and of brilliant victory alternating with humiliating compromise. The notable event took place on December 26, 1893, in Shaoshan, a little valley village sixty miles from Changsha, capital of Hunan Province.

At the hour of Mao's birth Sun Yat-sen was a twenty-seven-year-old doctor conspiring to overthrow the Manchu dynasty; Nikolai Lenin was a twenty-three-year-old law graduate beginning his career as a revolutionary in St. Petersburg; Joseph Stalin was a fourteen-year-old seminary student in Tiflis, furtively reading Charles Darwin in bed by candlelight; Chiang Kai-shek was a six-year-old helping his father, an impoverished salt merchant in east China; Franklin Delano Roosevelt was in a cradle at Hyde Park, New York; and Nikita Khrushchev lacked four months of being born.

The Mao family farmhouse stood apart from the dwellings of six hundred other families in the village, above two lotus-filled ponds on which ducks sailed serenely. Roofed partly with thatch and partly with round gray tiles, the house had a pigpen attached to one side. Mash for the hogs was prepared in a caldron in the kitchen on a long earthen stove, next to a huge cask for storing rice. Mao was born by oil lamp in a tiny "guest room" next to the pigsty.

His mother, Wen Ch'i-mei, was a gentle, oval-faced peasant woman who bore her husband three sons—Tse-tung, Tse-t'an, and Tse-min—and a daughter, Tse-hung. A devout Buddhist, she brought up her children in the faith. She worked hard for her family, cooking, keeping house, washing, caring for the livestock, gathering firewood, carrying water from the well, spinning cotton, mending and darning, working in the fields, and carrying loads of straw and manure on her shoulders.

When she failed to please her husband, he would beat her —a privilege accorded Chinese men by tradition.

Mao's father, Mao Jen-sheng, was a tall, strong peasant with a moustache and goatee, bushy eyebrows, and a long nose projecting over a hard mouth. In a land that almost every year knew famine he thought of nothing but his property, expanding it and squeezing and hoarding every penny he could.

He had begun life miserably poor and heavily in debt, but by sharp dealing in pigs and rice and giving his family barely enough to eat, he had managed to become a small landowner.

Mao's birth had greatly pleased him. Soon the child would be five—old enough to work in the fields with his mother and a hired hand. In the sowing and harvest seasons Mao Jen-sheng added extra laborers, attracting them to work in his terraced rice fields by serving luxury foods every fortnight—eggs, fish, and sometimes even meat. Of course, his wife and children never received anything but their small ration of unground rice and vegetables. One did not, after all, have to waste bribes on one's own family.

As Mao Tse-tung grew up, he came to fear and hate his penurious father, whom he called the Ruling Power. Mao Jen-sheng was greatly displeased by his son's attitude. Proper Chinese children displayed proper filial respect, bowing before their father's word as law. Stubborn children who balked or argued would unquestionably come to a bad end as bandits or other outcasts of society.

Mountainous Hunan in subtropical south China had the reputation of being a province of bandits and political rebels. The Hunanese were considered a hot-tempered, emotional, militaristic, heroic, upright, unyielding people in the forefront of every uprising. Tongue in cheek, Mao once attributed the Hunanese temperament to the red peppers they loved.

During his childhood, tremors began to shake the cruel, corrupt Manchu dynasty that had ruled China for three hundred years. The Chinese people felt humiliated by the foreign flags that the Manchus permitted to fly above imperialist compounds, by the foreign ships that dominated Chinese ports and rivers, by the foreign goods that flooded Chinese markets. Signs over legation clubs read: "FORBIDDEN TO DOGS AND CHINESE."

In 1894–1895 an unsuccessful war with Japan had forced the Empress Dowager Tz'u Hsi to surrender Formosa and Korea to Tokyo. Hatred of the foreigner reached a boiling point. A secret Chinese brotherhood called the Boxers vowed to unleash mob warfare against all white people in China.

At the turn of the century they struck. Missionaries and Christians were massacred; churches were burned; the legations in Peking were attacked and put under siege. The turmoil had little direct impact upon Mao, however, because he was only seven when the Boxer Rebellion erupted, and there were few Europeans in the Hunan region.

He had been working on his father's land for two years when Mao Jen-sheng, who was largely illiterate, decided that his son should learn to read and write in order to keep accounts and write letters for the family enterprise. So each morning after work in the fields young Mao would trot off to the village to attend Shaoshan's primary school, returning later in the day to resume labor in the rice terraces.

The pale-faced boy with thick black hair proved a poor scholar in English and arithmetic but won high marks in Chinese composition and debate. His teacher noted with approval his apparent absorption in the dull Confucian classics, unaware that hidden behind their covers were popular novels.

When Mao was ten, his teacher caught him savoring these secret delights one day and gave him a severe beating for ignoring his lessons. Outraged, Mao ran away from school.

Afraid of another beating from his father if he went home, he decided to make off through the mountains for the city of Changsha. For three days, hungry and exhausted, he stumbled blindly forward until he finally emerged into a clearing. Seeking food from some peasants working in their fields, he was shocked to find that they were from Shaoshan.

He was only three miles from home; he had traveled in circles. Turned over to his father, he dreaded the worst. But to his surprise, Mao Jen-sheng was so relieved to have him home that he even expressed grudging admiration for his son's proud spirit. Young Mao's teacher, too, was impressed with his "strike" against discipline and from that time on never laid hands upon him again. So at an early age Mao discovered that mistreatment did not have to be endured but that it could be mitigated by a touch of desperate and determined rebellion.

At thirteen he had had all the schooling his father deemed necessary. In 1906 he was put to work all day in the fields and at night computed the family accounts on an abacus.

His father was annoyed by his extravagant use of an oil lamp in his tiny room to read folk tales and historical novels long after everyone else was asleep. Mao's favorite books were *The Three Kingdoms,* a work of fiction exalting Confucian principles, and *Water Margin,* translated as *All Men Are Brothers* by Pearl Buck. The latter book told of heroic bandits who revolted against a corrupt court and bureaucracy, establishing themselves in a mountain fortress to fight for justice and order. This Chinese version of *Robin Hood* had a profound influence on Mao, who yearned to emulate its heroes.

When his father fumed at his "waste of valuable oil," he covered his window with blue cloth to conceal how long he pursued his habit of reading in bed. But Mao Senior was not deceived, and they quarreled about this and much else. Mao could never work long enough or hard enough or live penuriously enough to satisfy his mean-spirited father.

One evening his father denounced him in front of guests as a lazy, gluttonous boy guilty of unfilial conduct. Mao could bear no more. "Go to hell!" he shouted in blind rage.

The guests gasped. With an outraged roar Mao Jen-sheng lunged at his son, who fled outdoors to the edge of the pond. "I'll beat you to a pulp, you insolent whelp!"

"If you come near me," Mao vowed hysterically, "I shall throw myself in the pond!"

His father hesitated. "Apologize and kowtow, then!"

Mao considered the terms of amnesty. His offense had been outrageous in the China of that day. A son whose rebellion provoked his father's condemnation could not expect to find decent employment or social acceptance. Had Mao struck his father, Chinese law could even have condemned him to death. Nevertheless his spirit was too proud to submit fully to his father by kneeling before him.

"Confucius says elders must be kind and affectionate to the young," he reminded his father defiantly. "However, I will kowtow on *one* knee if you promise not to beat me."

Mao's compromise was enough to save face for his father before the guests, so Mao Jen-sheng agreed. Once more young Mao had found that spirited defiance in the face of authority earned more respect than abject submission to tyranny.

Emboldened, he now demanded to be allowed to continue his studies under an old scholar living in the village. His father fumed, but in the end Mao won his way and spent the next six months furthering his education.

His new studies taught him more about his country's accomplishments and problems. Mao took pride in the genius of Chinese inventors who had given the world paper, printing, books, gunpowder, the clock, and the compass. But he was depressed by the sad history of China ever since the Opium War.

He learned how defeat by Great Britain in 1842 had led to the Nanking Treaty ceding Hong Kong to the British and opening the ports of Canton, Shanghai, and other cities to foreign compounds, which in effect gave western nations control of China's major commerce. Following the costly defeat by Japan in 1894–1895, the last straw for many

Chinese had been the Russo-Japanese War ten years later. A defeated Russia had "granted" concessions and other "rights" in southern China to the victorious Japanese.

Mao wondered about the Russo-Japanese War. It marked the first time that a western power had been defeated by an Asian nation. If Japan could do it, why couldn't China also crush and throw out the western imperialists who squabbled over Chinese spoils like lions over a dying carcass?

Unknown to young Mao, Sun Yat-sen was forming a revolutionary Alliance Society in Tokyo. Sun's movement, Mao said later, was the beginning of the anti-imperialist, antifeudal, bourgeois democratic revolution that would convulse China for almost half a century. It sought to unite all the secret societies of China into one powerful national force to overthrow the Manchu dynasty as the slave of the western powers.

In 1906 Chinese unrest was heightened by a great flood in Hunan Province that caused widespread famine and suffering.

"Two miles outside my village," Mao later told André Malraux, French Minister of Culture under Charles de Gaulle, "there were trees stripped of their bark up to a height of twelve feet. Starving people had eaten it."

One day Mao and other village schoolboys were startled by a sudden influx of merchants from Changsha who bore alarming news. Starving people in the city, armed with pikes and pitchforks, had stormed government offices to demand food. The governor had ordered the execution of hundreds of rioters. Their heads had been chopped off and displayed on poles as a grim warning to other rice rioters. Mao was horrified.

But his father vehemently approved the governor's action. Mao Jen-sheng's own rice convoys sent to Changsha had been held up and robbed by famished villagers. His son hesitated to approve such drastic solutions to China's age-old scourge. But what other answer was there?

Young Mao was made thoughtful by a book called *Words of Warning,* which attributed China's misfortunes to her lack of modern development in a world dominated by an industrially powerful West. He was also alarmed by a pamphlet, "On China's Danger of Being Dismembered by Foreign Powers," which began with the mournful prophecy "Alas, China will be subjugated."

Anxious for the future of his country, he burned with a patriotic zeal to save it. But his father now insisted that he terminate his studies and return to work full-time, weeding the fields, looking after livestock, and keeping the books. By this time, despite his meager diet, fourteen-year-old Mao was almost as tall and strong as his father.

In accordance with Chinese custom his parents selected a wife for him, and in 1907 Mao married a girl four years older than himself. After the ceremony he drew aside her veil, found her anything but attractive, and refused to abide as her husband. Later he repudiated the marriage. The experience embittered him against all arranged marriages.

Friction mounted between Mao and his father. One autumn when the rains came early, instead of helping to collect his father's thrashed rice in the granary, he aided his father's poor tenants with theirs instead. His father refused to speak to him for days.

When he was sixteen, his father sought to apprentice him to a rice shop merchant, but by now Mao was determined to pursue studies that would teach him how he could help save his country from disaster. Borrowing from friends and relatives, he raised enough money to defray the cost of attending Tungshan High School in his mother's hometown, Siangsiang.

His father's reaction was frosty. "It is not enough to pay only for this whim of yours. You must also pay for the laborer I must hire to take your place in the fields."

A cousin lent Mao the necessary annual wage for a field hand—twelve dollars. Then, packing his blue mosquito net, a pair of sheets, some clothes, and his two favorite books, Mao slung his bundle over his shoulder and happily trudged the thirteen miles to Siangsiang.

He was awed by his year at Tungshan High, a modern school surrounded by a moat crossed by a white stone bridge. Until now he had lived in a world where almost everyone was dirt poor or a notch or two above that level, like his father.

Now for the first time he came into contact with finely dressed, beautifully spoken sons of landlords who were amused at the oversize boy in a frayed jacket and trousers made out of rough, blue-dyed cloth. All were as much as six years younger, their schooling uninterrupted by work in rice fields.

Mao cut such an awkward, grotesque figure among his classmates that most could not resist ridiculing him. He had been admitted only because his mother had been a resident of Siangsiang. Mao reacted by roughing up the worst offenders and behaving toward others with a stubborn arrogance. He would not let any see how deeply his feelings had been wounded.

But one day the landlord class of China would have good reason to regret that their sons at Siangsiang had not been kinder to their classmate, Mao Tse-tung.

# Chapter 2

# "Beat the Slaves of Foreigners!"

Mao nevertheless made a few close friends at school. He also impressed his teachers by his ability to write thoughtful essays and sensitive poetry. A book called *Great Heroes of the World* introduced him to Napoleon, Peter the Great, Abraham Lincoln, Jean Jacques Rousseau, William Gladstone, Catherine the Great, and George Washington. He was fascinated by the Washington story because it seemed to him that what China now needed was an Oriental George Washington.

"Washington won victory and built up his nation," Mao told his friends thoughtfully, "only after eight long, bitter years of war." Was that, he wondered, the path for China?

He became more and more fascinated by the lives of warriors and nation-builders. Half a century later he revealed to a visiting French delegation that as a schoolboy he had respected Maximilien Robespierre as a revolutionary but had actually been more impressed by Napoleon as a nation-builder.

Schooling at Siangsiang intensified his compassion for the suffering of his countrymen. Returning home for the holidays, he collected debts for his father during another famine but one day turned all the money he had collected over to a group of homeless peasants he encountered. On his way back to school, overtaking a threadbare student in a snowstorm, he threw his own cloak around the shivering boy's shoulders.

In 1911 he won admission into Hsianghsiang Middle School in Changsha and jubilantly took a steamboat down the Hsiang River. He immediately visited the Hunan Provincial Library, where he saw an astonishing sight—a map of the world.

Fascinated, he studied the shape, size, and position of China in relation to the rest of the world. His schooling up to now had deceived him, Mao decided; China certainly was *not* the center of the world. Huge, it certainly was—but how small compared to the rest of the world!

The library's thousands of volumes sparked an impulsive decision. Instead of attending the Middle School, he would spend every day in this magic world of forbidden knowledge, reading wherever his curiosity led him—politics, economics, history, geography.

"I went to the library in the morning when it opened," he later recalled. "At noon I paused only long enough to buy and consume two rice cakes, which were my daily lunch. I stayed in the library every day reading until it closed."

He was sustained, but barely, in this program of self-education by a miserly allowance from his father, who imagined that he was at school. Mao lodged austerely at a boardinghouse with other students and unemployed soldiers, between whom there was considerable bad blood.

One day a group of intoxicated soldiers attacked the students. Mao's long legs served him in good stead, and he managed to escape a beating by hiding out in the rest room.

The library led him to another fascinating discovery—*People's Strength,* the first newspaper he had ever read. It told him that seventy-two Cantonese had been killed in an uprising against the Manchus and that the Dowager Empress had died two years earlier. Mao marveled at the wonderful idea of a printed gossip that told you everything going on in the world locally and nationally. Without newspapers no wonder rural peasants were still living in the eighteenth and nineteenth centuries!

He was fascinated on October 10, 1911, when *People's Strength* revealed that Sun Yat-sen had signaled the outbreak of full-scale revolution with a bomb blast in Hangkow. The Manchu dynasty had immediately arrested supporters of Sun and executed them publicly as traitors. A section of the army had revolted, and teachers and students all over China were organizing mass meetings to support Sun's revolution.

"China has fallen to the lowest place among the nations," Sun broadcast from Tokyo. "We are four hundred millions on an immense territory, but our government does not govern. The court sells positions and dignities, the nobles and mandarins are also all for sale, and brigands are everywhere unchecked. . . .

"Japan required only a few decades in the school of the Europeans and Americans to become one of the great powers of the world. China has a population ten times greater and a territory thirty times larger than Japan. If China imitates Japan, she will become as strong as ten great powers."

Sun urged the creation of a Chinese democratic republic with a Confucian brand of mild socialism. Within a few days Manchu governors had been driven from a number of cities.

Now almost eighteen, Mao was caught up in the revolutionary fervor that swept the country. Here, at last, was the hope of a China saved from the gloomy prediction that haunted him persistently: "Alas, China will be subjugated. . . ."

Lettering posters with messages like "OUT WITH THE

MANCHUS" and "SET CHINA FREE," he pasted them on Changsha walls. He cut off his pigtail, symbol of subservience to the Emperor, and urged other students to follow suit. A dozen who promised reneged out of fear. Mao and a friend clipped their queues forcibly.

When the revolutionary army reached and took Changsha, Mao eagerly enlisted. He was made an officers' orderly. Required to fetch water for the officers' mess, Mao felt that this chore was demeaning to an intellectual. Hiring a water peddler to perform the service for him, he paid for it out of his meager soldier's salary of seven dollars a month.

"I used to feel it undignified to do any manual labor," he recalled later. "It seemed to me that the intellectuals were the only clean persons in the world, and the workers and peasants seemed rather dirty beside them. . . . But after a while in the same ranks as workers and peasants of the revolutionary army . . . a fundamental change occurred in the feelings implanted in me by the bourgeois schools. I came to feel that . . . the workers and peasants were after all the cleanest . . . even though their hands were soiled and their feet smeared with manure."

Mao was moved by his illiterate comrades' awe of his ability to read and write. He wrote letters home for them, read the replies, and told them the news in the press.

Nanking had fallen to Sun Yat-sen's forces, and China's two-thousand-year-old monarchy had come to an abrupt end. A Chinese Republic had been declared, minus Mongolia and Tibet, which had broken away as independent nations. The new flag flying over China showed a rising sun, symbolizing the dawn of a new day. Sun Yat-sen, a mild Cantonese intellectual in a stiff collar and soft hat, had been named provisional President.

Sun's fine words soon melted in the furnace of military realities. The real strong man of China was powerful General Yuan Shih-k'ai, a former imperialist who controlled the north. Yuan threatened civil war if Sun did not step aside for him. Sun conferred anxiously with leaders of his Kuomintang (National People's party). They agreed it would be best for Sun to yield to Yuan, who then became the new President.

To Sun's dismay Yuan promptly outlawed the Kuomintang, intending to revive the Manchu dynasty with himself as the new Emperor. But three months later he suddenly died. Hundreds of regional warlords—self-styled generals —began fighting among themselves for territory and power. So great was the chaos that Sun was forced to flee for his life to Japan, where he vainly pleaded for western support.

Meanwhile Mao, after six dull months as an orderly, resigned from the army. Undecided about his future, he registered in turn at a police school, a soap-making school, a law school, and a commercial school. None of these appealed to him, and he finally decided to become a teacher. After all, what greater contribution could he make to the new China than molding the minds of youth to win them for Sun's ideals? Besides, teaching would leave him time for reading widely.

So at the age of nineteen, with his father's permission, Mao sought to prepare himself for a career in the academic world. Taking an entrance examination for the Teachers Training School in Changsha, he passed so brilliantly that he won free tuition and cheap board between 1912 and 1917.

Now, seeking to unlock the secrets of western progress, he thoughtfully analyzed Adam Smith, Herbert Spencer, and Charles Darwin. His papers on them irritated one professor for a petty reason—Mao's habit of concluding each paper with the date. Ordered to stop it, Mao refused. When he turned in his next paper, the angry professor ripped out and crumpled the last page.

Mao's proud nature had changed little from the days of his student "strike." Gripping the professor's arm, he sought to drag him to the headmaster's office to argue the matter. The startled instructor had second thoughts, offering to let Mao continue to date his papers, provided he would recopy the crumpled page and say no more of the matter.

His point won, Mao cordially agreed. He was now more convinced than ever of the value of firm defiance in the face of an arbitrary exercise of authority. In 1912, despite threats of expulsion, he organized a student union that struck for better meals and a relaxation of irksome regulations, and won.

No rabble-rouser, Mao was now a quiet, serious youth of few words who preferred listening to talking. His four hundred classmates voted him one of the school's "model students," based on points for ethical behavior, self-control, courage, ability, and excellence in speech and literature.

When other students needed help in conflicts with authority, they turned to Mao. Once a classmate found himself being forced into an arranged marriage he hated to the niece of a school headmaster and begged Mao to get him out of it. Spurred by his own unhappy memories, Mao called on the headmaster, arguing so forcefully that he won freedom for his fellow student.

One of his great discoveries at the Teachers Training School was a book called *A System of Ethics*. Its author, Friedrich Paulsen, argued that all obstacles, personal and national, could be overcome by the development of sheer willpower and determination. Impressed, Mao scribbled his reflections in the margins of the book:

> In the past I worried over the coming destruction of our country, but now I know that fear was unnecessary. I have no doubt that the political system, the characteristics of our people, and the society

> will change; what I am not yet clear about are the ways in which
> the changes can be successfully brought about. . . . Let destruction
> play the role of a mother in giving birth to a new country. The great
> revolutions of other countries in the past centuries swept away the
> old and brought forth the new.

One of two instructors who made a deep impression upon Mao was Hsü T'e-li, who had studied in Japan with Sun. Hsü manifested great scorn for ostentation by deliberately coming to school on foot, instead of in rickshas or sedan chairs like other teachers. Mao never forgot Hsü's object lesson in demonstrated humility. No matter how high he climbed, he always dressed and lived like a simple peasant.

His search for a dynamic philosophy was aided by his professor of ethics, Yang Ch'ang-chi, who taught him how to blend the best ideas of East and West. Mao was warned not to seek a substitute culture, but to cherish China's own heritage while learning how to prod it into the twentieth century by applying western science and technology.

Mao's admiration for Yang extended to his pretty daughter, Yang K'ai-hui, a small, round-faced girl with white skin and deep-set eyes. Well educated but shy, she never spoke at table when her father invited his brightest students to lunch, but Mao lost his heart to her at first sight.

Her father imbued him with scorn for those Chinese who were subservient toward the West. Once Mao attended a soccer match between the Teachers Training School and Yale in China, a preparatory school for the sons of Chinese linked to the western settlements in China. Rising in the stands, tall and conspicuous, he bellowed through cupped hands: *"Beat the slaves of foreigners!"*

Yang taught Mao to blame the country's technological backwardness for the profound misery in which most Chinese lived. In the coalfields near Peking the production rate

was about 1 percent of that in America. And to achieve that
1 percent, small naked boys cut coal from mine faces and
were harnessed to heavy basketloads which they dragged
up to the surface on all fours, like dray horses. The children
worked twelve hours a day, seven days a week. They won
free coffins when they died.

A later poem reflected Mao's musings in 1917 as he
sought to identify the source of China's suffering:

> I opened the window of a solitary tower
> And asked: Who, on this enormous planet,
> Decides the destiny of human beings?

His first published attempt to improve the lot of his fellow Chinese was an article in 1917 in the magazine *New
Youth,* founded by Ch'en Tu-hsiu, a Marxist college dean
in Shanghai. Called "A Study of Physical Culture," it urged
his readers to go in for body-building exercises.

"The physical condition of the population deteriorates
daily," Mao deplored. "This is an extremely disturbing
phenomenon. . . . If our bodies are not strong, we will be
afraid as soon as we see enemy soldiers, and then how can
we attain our goals and make ourselves respected?"

Mao practiced what he preached, living a rugged, Spartan life in accord with Professor Yang's exhortation: "Every
day one must do something difficult to strengthen one's
will." Like Yang, he began each morning, summer or winter, with a cold tub bath.

In the summer of 1916 he and a friend, Siao Yu, decided
to get to know the problems of Hunanese peasants firsthand
by hiking across the whole province. Mao carried only an
umbrella, a change of clothes, a towel, a notebook, a writing brush, and an ink box. The young wanderers begged
their food, meeting with great kindness from the peasants.
Many, however, were too poor to offer them more than

beans and water. Departing after a night's hospitality, Mao would present their hosts with a gift of scrolls done in his beautiful calligraphy.

During another summer Mao and two other friends, Ts'ai Ho-sheng and Chang Kun-ti, imitated other ascetic practices of Professor Yang by living in a hut high on Yuehlu Mountain. Every morning they would come down for a swim in the river, then climb back up to meditate, take sun or wind baths, or run naked in the rain. They lived on only one meal a day, and that was merely broad beans.

Until late fall they would swim in the ice-tinged river, climb the mountain to sleep in the frost, and shout aloud on the mountaintop poems they had written in exhilarated praise of living close to nature. Mao wrote:

> To struggle against Heaven, what joy!
> To struggle against Earth, what joy!

The rugged conditioning of his body as a young man undoubtedly later helped him survive the brutal ordeal of the famous Long March that killed all but a handful of the toughest Chinese who undertook it. Increasingly, Mao grew to think of strength itself as a virtue. Two new names went on his list of personal heroes—Otto von Bismarck and Wilhelm II, the German Kaiser, whom Mao now admired as "strong men."

In 1917 the Teachers Training School was threatened with disruption by raging battles between northern warlords and Kwangsi troops of the south loyal to the Kuomintang. School authorities panicked when they heard that some retreating detachments of warlord Fu Liang-tso were planning to commandeer the school as their headquarters.

Mao volunteered to raise a force of the most athletic students to defend the school. Deferred to as an army veteran, he drilled both students and professors, who respected his leadership and obeyed his orders. To keep Fu Liang-tso's troops from climbing over the school wall, he set up sharp bamboo stakes outside it. All school doors were barricaded with furniture.

Securing some rifles and medical supplies from the local police, Mao led a small band of youths to a hiding spot on a nearby mountain. That night an advance echelon of Fu Liang-tso's forces was spotted headed for the school. Mao led his small force down the dark mountain. Near the road he shouted fiercely, "Fu Liang-tso has fled! Kwangsi troops have entered Changsha! Surrender! Surrender!" Then they charged.

Frightened troops of the warlord fled. It was Mao's first military victory, and he was thrilled.

At the end of the school year most students went home, but Mao, as usual, did not. His affection for his mother was outweighed by his hostility toward his father. Feeling lonely, he put ads in the Changsha papers admitting, "The oriole is chirping, looking for friends"—a classic expression indicating the need of companionship. He urged young men who were "hardened and determined, and ready to make sacrifices for their country" to get in touch with "28 Strokes"—the number required to write Mao's name in Chinese.

He was surprised and gratified by the response. Soon he had a New People's Study Society organized to find ways to demolish the "four evil demons of empire"—repression of the individual in the name of Confucian piety; religion; capitalism; autocracy. Many members of the society later followed Mao into the Communist party. Most were fated to meet death at the hands of Chiang Kai-shek.

When Mao's years at the Teachers Training School drew to a close in April, 1918, many events had focused simultaneously to dictate his next move. The October, 1917, Bolshevik Revolution in Russia had stirred the world.

Marxist study societies in China had sprung up everywhere.

Mao's home ties now withered almost completely with the death of his mother. He threw himself into furthering a new long-range revolutionary strategy. France, suffering a labor shortage during World War I, had devised a "work and study" scheme to recruit Chinese labor. Mao helped organize work-study groups from Changsha, hopeful that they would return with a knowledge of French science and technology as well as of the agitation techniques of French labor.

Mao's friend Siao Yu urged him to join the Chinese contingents bound for France. Mao refused, not only because he was reluctant to leave the Chinese soil he loved, but also because of his secret love for Yang K'ai-hui. He agreed to accompany Siao Yu to Peking, however, because Professor Yang and his lovely daughter had transferred to the university there.

Yang welcomed him enthusiastically. His daughter's warm glances left little doubt about her attraction to the tall, thin, handsome twenty-five-year-old youth with raven-black hair, dreamy romantic black eyes beneath majestic brows, and a charming, gentle smile.

Professor Yang introduced Mao to the librarian of Peking University, Li Ta-chao, who agreed to hire him to work in the stacks at eight dollars a month with the grandiloquent title of "Assistant Librarian." It was a humble job, and Mao later recalled that he had been thoroughly ignored by important intellectuals who had used the library.

He joined seven other young men in renting a two-room house they could not afford to heat. Sleeping huddled with the others for warmth, Mao had to warn those on each side of him when he wanted to turn over. But there were compensations. He loved Peking's beautiful parks and old palace grounds, the autumn song of cicadas in the orchards, willows draped in winter's ice crystals. Best of all, there were talks with Yang K'ai-hui.

Mao was intrigued in the spring of 1918 when a Society for the Study of Marxism was formed at the University of Peking by his librarian boss, Li Ta-chao, and the editor of *New Youth,* Ch'en Tu-hsiu. Joining, Mao read for the first time Karl Marx's *The Communist Manifesto,* just translated into Chinese.

Deeply impressed, Mao agreed that only the Chinese masses could overthrow the warlords. But why did Marx stress only the importance of uprisings by city workers and neglect the revolutionary role of the peasants? Mao's baffled question was to prove the greatest thorn of contention not only within the ranks of Chinese Marxists, but also between the Soviet Union and China for the next half century.

# Chapter 3

# Working with Chiang

Paradoxically, the further Marxism took him toward communal thinking, the more of an individualist Mao became. He was now in full revolt against Confucian doctrines demanding respect for parental and political authority. Instead of being manipulated from above, Mao insisted, one should be one's own taskmaster, doing what is required voluntarily by self-discipline and strength of will.

"There can be no greater crime," he wrote in 1918, "than repression of the individual."

Early in 1919 he applied for and won a job editing a Hunan student journal, *Hsiang River Review,* in Changsha. He lost no time stirring up rebellion against the old order.

"What is the greatest force?" he wrote. "The greatest force is that of the union of the popular masses. What should we not fear? We should not fear heaven. We should not fear ghosts. We should not fear the dead. We should not fear the bureaucrats. We should not fear the militarists. We should not fear the capitalists."

The governor of Hunan, warlord General Chang Ching-yao, did not take kindly to Mao's inflammatory views. *Hsiang River Review* came to an abrupt end with its fifth issue.

Undaunted, Mao accepted the editorship of another student weekly, *New Hunan.* Moved by the suicide of a young

Hunan girl whose parents had forced her to marry against her will, he wrote nine slashing attacks on the Establishment.

Emancipate men and women, Mao cried, from the bondage of traditional Confucian thought and institutions! Down with restraints on the liberty of the individual! Make way for a "great wave of the freedom to love"! Chang Ching-yao abruptly shut down *New Hunan.*

Mao now organized a United Students' Association and led demonstrations protesting the kowtowing of the national government to Japan's land grab of Shantung. He also organized a boycott of Japanese goods. Infuriated, Chang Ching-yao summoned Mao and other student leaders, warning them hysterically to stop meddling in the politics of their elders.

"If you don't listen to me," he screamed, "I'll cut off your heads!" Scenes like this, later charged his successor, proved that Chang was "not a man but a wild beast."

A frightened girl student began to cry. "Pay no more attention to him," Mao whispered to her, "than you would to a barking dog."

In December, 1919, he organized a strike of all Hunan students against the governor and forced Chang Ching-yao to make some concessions. When the strike was over, Mao prudently decided to leave Changsha before the barking dog bit.

He went to Shanghai for long, thoughtful discussions with Ch'en Tu-hsiu, cofounder of the Society for the Study of Marxism, about the best way to struggle against the old order. Ch'en had just emerged from six months in jail for supporting student demonstrations. Mao took a job as a laundryman while in Shanghai, during which time Ch'en fully converted him to the Marxist point of view.

Early in 1920 Governor Chang Ching-yao was driven out of Hunan by Kuomintang forces. One of Mao's former teachers in Changsha, I P'ei-chi, was named director of the Teachers Training School. He promptly appointed laundryman Mao a professor as well as director of the primary school.

Mao at once returned to Changsha, eager to utilize his new opportunities to promote revolutionary goals. He had now moved far beyond the point of believing that liberation for the Chinese people could be won merely by destroying the authority system of Confucianism. China would not be free, he was now convinced, until a Marxist government took power, as in Russia, crushing domestic reactionaries and driving out foreign oppressors—Japan along with the western nations.

By October he had organized the nucleus of a Changsha Communist party. By December he began recruiting students into a Socialist Youth Corps.

In the winter of 1921–1922, feeling economically secure enough for the first time, he married the daughter of his revered Professor Yang Ch'ang-chi, who had recently died. Pretty Yang K'ai-hui soon presented Mao with two children, both boys. They saw little of their father, however, as Mao became more deeply involved in conspiratorial activities.

By the spring of 1921 there were five other functioning Communist groups in China besides the one under Mao in Changsha. In Paris Chou En-lai had also formed a Communist party of Chinese working in France.

The Comintern, operating from Moscow, now decided that it was time to unite these groups into a national Chinese Communist party (CCP) and sent a Dutch agent to help organize it. Each city group on the Chinese mainland sent two delegates to meet with him in Shanghai. They gathered at a private girls' school, closed for the holidays, chosen in the hope of escaping government observation.

But Mao quickly spotted secret police. At his suggestion

the thirteen conspirators entrained to a lake where they hired a boat and packed food and wine for an outing. Out of that placid "picnic" of a handful of dedicated revolutionaries came the great cataclysmic changes that would soon sweep a nation of seven hundred million people and shake the world in the process.

The new national CCP decided to adopt the theory and techniques of the successful Russian Communist party in seeking to make China a classless society. Mao was still bothered by the Russian view that communism could only be brought about by the proletariat, or urban working class. In Russia perhaps this was true. But before Chinese society could be changed, the people and their attitudes would first have to be changed—and the vast majority of Chinese were peasants. Yet who was he to question Lenin, Leon Trotsky, and Stalin, who had made Marxism work?

Named CCP Secretary for Hunan Province, Mao developed a front group for revolutionary activity, the Changsha Self-Study University. Those who joined were encouraged to study ways in which the best in Chinese thought might be combined with the principles of Marxism. But Mao soon made it clear that they were also expected to translate ideas into action.

"Capitalism cannot be overthrown," he wrote to a friend in France, "by small pressures restricted to the field of education." Elected chairman of the Hunan Association of Trade Unions, Mao organized mine and railroad strikes.

The new governor of Hunan, Chao Heng-t'i, was greatly upset. "As long as Mao Tse-tung is in Hunan," he declared, "there can be no room for me."

Recruiting members for the CCP in backward, illiterate China proved a discouraging business. By June, 1922, the party still had only three hundred members, 90 percent of them intellectuals and only 10 percent workers. Mao was the sole member with a peasant background. How could they attract and win over the poor masses who couldn't read party propaganda?

Mao formed a Cultural Book Society, ostensibly to teach illiterate adults a basic one-thousand-character vocabulary. But eschewing standard texts, he wrote and prepared special beginners' manuals. These taught, along with phonetics, that the wealth of a nation was produced by workers and peasants and explained what they had accomplished in the Soviet Union.

Through sympathetic contacts he managed to have his manuals distributed throughout Hunan by members of the Chinese YMCA, which was supported by American funds. Outraged, Governor Chao Heng-t'i ordered Mao's arrest as a radical.

Mao fled to Shanghai. At the Third CCP Congress his growing reputation won him election to the Central Committee as chief of the party's organizing bureau.

China, meanwhile, was being run by northern warlords with fat loans from western nations. Sun Yat-sen, still in exile abroad, grimly realized that his appeals for support to foreign democracies were futile. "The prevailing estimate of Dr. Sun," said *The New York Times,* "has been that he is a dreamer and therefore dangerous."

The western powers preferred a weakened China torn by civil war. By bribing the warlords they could assure protection for their highly profitable extraterritorial holdings and concessions. Why support a Sun Yat-sen who had strongly nationalistic and socialistic views?

Sun finally turned, reluctantly, to the only country now willing to help him—the Soviet Union. Definitely sympathetic, Lenin was also interested in extending the boundaries of communism. An understanding was reached.

Returning to Canton, Sun managed to reorganize his shaky Chinese Republic in 1921 by making a deal with local southern warlords. He now signified his new militancy by dressing in the uniform, sword, and plumed cap of a genera-lissimo for his inauguration as President of the Republic.

It was soon pathetically apparent, however, that he was incapable of imposing his authority upon a nation divided into a dozen or more *de facto* states run by feudal warlords. Their power would have to be broken before anything like a real Chinese nation could be created.

When Chinese CCP delegates went to Moscow in 1922 to attend the First Congress of the Toilers of the Far East, they had a surprise awaiting them. Comintern chief Grigori Zinoviev upbraided them for the failure of the Chinese Reds to support Sun. The CCP, he insisted, must form an alliance with the Kuomintang (KMT) and help Sun free China of the northern warlords and their western support-ers.

Soon afterward a Soviet envoy to Sun in Canton pledged Russian help in building a strong Nationalist army. The Third CCP Congress then voted to join the KMT "as in-dividuals."

"The Kuomintang," agreed Mao and other CCP leaders, "must be the central force in the national revolution, and assume the leadership of the revolution." A United Front had been born in China.

Sun Yat-sen now advocated socialism in three stages: first nationalism, then democracy, and finally socialism. "We have lost hope of help from America, England, France," he told *The New York Times* in 1923. ". . . The only country that shows any sign of helping us in the South is the Soviet Government." In October Moscow sent black-moustached Michael Borodin to Canton to act as Sun's political adviser, accompanied by military adviser General Vasili Bluecher, better known under his alias of Galin.

A key figure in the new alliance was Sun's chief of staff, young Colonel Chiang Kai-shek, who had won Sun's confi-dence as his military aide in Japan. The slim, stern-faced

Chiang had a personal antipathy for communism but could not help admiring the way in which the Soviet Red Army had won and enlisted the support of the Russian people.

In 1923 Sun sent him to Moscow, where Lenin now lay dying, to study Soviet military methods. He returned a year later to help Borodin and Galin organize the Whampoa Military Academy, equipped and staffed by Kremlin experts. Chiang, now thirty-seven, was named Commandant, with twenty-five-year-old Chou En-lai as his political commissar. They began training officers for a modern national army.

One of the earliest graduates was Lin Piao, eighteen-year-old son of a textile-factory owner ruined by warlord "taxation." Lin's record at the academy was a brilliant one. His campaigns against the warlords soon afterward were so successful that he had achieved the rank of colonel by his twentieth birthday.

Mao had now transferred his organizational talents to the Shanghai bureau of the KMT, where he worked long and hard on behalf of Dr. Sun. Not all his comrades in the CCP shared his enthusiasm for the United Front. Some suspected Sun—correctly—of seeking to make secret deals with northern warlords. They also distrusted Chiang Kai-shek as an ambitious warlord type who would sell out to the vested interests of China as soon as he had the power to do so.

The dissidents attacked the United Front policy at CCP meetings. Their spokesman was Li Li-san, an old comrade of Mao's from Changsha. He criticized Mao bitterly for playing into the hands of the KMT. Mao, upset and worn out from years of overwork, decided to take a leave of absence. He returned to his native village of Shaoshan, hopeful that the idyllic peace of the countryside would soothe his raw nerves.

In March, 1925, a paralyzed, almost blind Sun Yat-sen, in the midst of negotiations with northern warlords, died of cancer. He left a letter addressed to Stalin: "In turning their eyes toward you, the millions of men enslaved beneath the yoke of imperialism will rekindle the flame of hope, and the courage that will sustain them."

On the advice of Borodin and Galin, Chiang Kai-shek was made the new Commander in Chief with the rank of Generalissimo. He soon revealed a dictatorial nature, permitting no discussion of any of his decisions.

An event in May, 1925, set all China aflame with anger at foreign autonomy on Chinese soil. When Shanghai students demonstrated in sympathy with a strike against a Japanese-owned factory, police of the International Settlement shot and killed ten, wounding fifty others. Rioting broke out in other cities. In Canton British and French police fired into crowds, killing fifty-two more Chinese. Half a million workers now went on strike, protesting the right of foreign powers to murder Chinese people on Chinese soil.

But the western powers could not be driven out of China, Mao was convinced, until their northern warlord puppets were first crushed. Accepting a job editing the *Political Weekly* for the KMT, he urged the peasantry to give full support to Chiang Kai-shek's Nationalist Liberation Expedition, soon to be sent north against half a million troops of the warlords.

To provide a political cadre of peasants who would organize the countryside for the expedition, he opened a Peasant Movement Training Institute. His younger brother Mao Tse-min attended as a student. The cadre were taught to persuade peasants that only by uniting behind KMT forces could they get rid of the warlords, win ownership of the land they tilled, and become masters in their own country.

Li Li-san now attacked Mao's preoccupation with the peasantry as a Marxist "deviation." Had not Marx declared that the revolution could be won only in the cities? The peasants were petty bourgeois better left to the KMT. All CCP members should concentrate on organizing the proletariat. Mao was saddened when Ch'en Tu-hsiu, his old mentor in Marxism, joined Li Li-san in criticizing him.

The CCP faction led by Li and Ch'en strongly distrusted Chiang Kai-shek and wanted to pull out of the United Front. But in October, 1925, they were overruled by Borodin, Stalin's representative in China. This struggle within the CCP did not go unreported to Chiang. Right-wing elements of the KMT urged him to expel the Communists.

Mao was under no illusions about the ultimate goals of the bourgeois in the United Front. He knew that as soon as the Nationalist struggle became a class struggle—as the CCP would see that it did—the right wing of the United Front would go over to the imperialist camp.

"As to the vacillating middle class," he warned in March, 1926, "its right wing may become our enemy, and its left wing may become our friend." The danger of a premature split in the United Front, as Mao saw it, was that chaos would overtake China before it had been freed from the grip of the warlords. Events one year later were to prove him correct.

In July, 1926, Mao and the Li–Ch'en faction reached a compromise. Ties between the CCP and KMT would be loosened but not severed. At the same time Mao would be allowed to continue organizing the peasantry as head of a CCP Peasant Department; not merely for Chiang's forces, however, but also to win their primary loyalty to the CCP in areas that would be occupied by Nationalist troops.

To head his cadres in the field, Mao sent a special task force headed by flat-nosed Chu Teh, a former warlord turned Communist. Chu sped north ahead of KMT troops to inflame the countryside against landlordism and feudalism.

On July 9, 1926, the Nationalist Army marched out of

the pale-yellow rice fields surrounding Canton, and the Northern Expedition was finally under way. At first they found themselves welcomed and helped everywhere. It had not been difficult for Chu Teh's cadres to mobilize peasants against the hated warlord armies that swarmed across the land.

The warlords were land pirates who preyed on the people with private armies, treating them brutally and robbing them in the guise of taxes. Some warlords respected each other's territories; others fought each other for spoils, and peasants were often victimized by both rival warlords.

By August all of Hunan was in the hands of Chiang's forces. Warlords' troops had little reason to love their brutal masters or remain loyal to them, and many defected to the Nationalists. Before the end of the year the KMT had more than doubled the size of its forces. Many recruits were peasants eager for a chance to fight back against their oppressors.

Chiang followed his troops north in a headquarters train, accompanied by Stalin's envoy, Borodin, and his Russian staff. Among the CCP representatives on the train was Mao Tse-tung, who was now directing Chu Teh's agitation campaign as "Chief of the KMT Propaganda Department."

He was still resentful of Chinese intellectuals like Li Lisan and Ch'en Tu-hsiu for looking down upon the huge illiterate peasantry as a revolutionary liability. Peasant poverty and ignorance, as Mao saw it, were potential assets. Their lot was so desperate that they would gladly fight for *any* change in their plight. And they had no preconceived political prejudices, so that whoever changed their lives for the better would win their hearts and minds forever.

Whatever Mao's political rivals in the CCP may have thought of his ideology, none questioned his personal integrity. He had no desire to exploit the misery of the peasantry merely as a ladder to seize power for himself. He genuinely sought to raise them up by education and socialism to become a great and happy people. Of course one day idealistic Chinese youth might find inspiration in reading about *him*—the Communist hero who had rescued them from warlords and imperialists. He was human enough to enjoy that daydream.

Mao's campaign to stir the countryside was aided by a bad harvest that had created famine conditions. Encouraged by Chu's task force, peasant revolts began flaring up through Hunan like a string of huge firecrackers, one explosion touching off another. Chiang's troops, fanning out in victorious occupation, found more antifeudalism than they could handle.

Peasants smashed aside local police and raided the silos of big landowners. Merchants who refused to give alms to the starving were beaten in their sedan chairs. Mobs broke into the yards of landlords to slaughter pigs for food; some hated landlords were put to death. Unpopular officials were arrested, forced to wear dunce caps, roped together, and paraded through villages. Many upper-class Chinese fled the reign of terror in Hunan, and their lands were confiscated.

KMT troops arriving in these areas were shocked by wild spectacles of anarchy and rebellion. Most officers were sons of middle-class merchants, landlords, and officials. Filing bitter complaints with Chiang, KMT commanders accused the Communists of "treason" in stirring these uprisings.

Mao was delighted. "In a very short time," he predicted, "several million peasants in China's central, southern and northern provinces will rise like a tornado or tempest—a force so extraordinarily swift and violent that no power, however great, will be able to suppress it." He visualized the swift replacement of the feudal landlord class by peasant soviets all over China.

The CCP Central Committee was impressed, and for

once Mao's critics were silent. He was sent on a tour of inspection of Hunan to report on conditions. Wherever he traveled, small landlords and "middle" farmers begged him to win entry for them into the new peasant associations they had originally scoffed at and refused to join.

"What was looked down upon four months ago as a 'gang of peasants' has now become a most honorable institution," Mao observed in satisfaction. "Those who formerly prostrated themselves before the power of the gentry now bow before the power of the peasants. . . . All admit that the world since last October is a different one."

Mao could scarcely be blamed for believing that his double role, as official propagandist for the KMT and secret rabble-rouser for the CCP, was the magic key for destroying, at one and the same time, the power of the warlords and the bourgeois aspirations of Chiang Kai-shek. He now set about proving it to his dubious city-minded comrades in the CCP.

# Chapter 4

# Treachery in Shanghai

In February, 1927, sequestered in a confiscated house shaded by poinsettia and beech-trees, Mao wrote his famous *Report Concerning and Inquiry into the Peasant Movement in the Province of Hunan.* The poor, illiterate peasant masses, he now insisted, were the most effective revolutionary force in China, whether the urban intellectuals of the CCP Central Committee were willing to recognize this fact or not. Constituting 70 percent of China's population, if they but sneezed in unison, they would blow away the other 30 percent.

"The privileges which the feudal landlords have enjoyed for thousands of years are being shattered to pieces," he pointed out. "Every bit of the dignity and prestige built up by the landlords is being swept into the dust. . . . The popular slogan 'All power to the peasant associations' has become a reality." He then addressed himself to charges by KMT bourgeois that what was going on was "terrible."

"In a few months the peasants have accomplished what Dr. Sun Yat-sen wanted, but failed, to accomplish in the forty years he devoted to the national revolution. This is a marvelous feat never before achieved, not just in forty, but in thousands of years. It's fine. It's not 'terrible' at all."

What reactionaries called "going too far," Mao insisted, was actually a mighty revolutionary upsurge to give peasants power over their own lives. "What the peasants are doing is absolutely right. . . . The local tyrants, evil gentry and lawless landlords have themselves driven the peasants to this. . . . A revolution is not a dinner party, or writing an essay, or painting a picture, or doing embroidery."

Far from being anything so refined, he added, "it was necessary to overthrow the whole authority of the gentry, to strike them to the ground and keep them there . . . necessary to create terror for a while in every rural area. . . . All those whom the gentry had despised, those whom they had trodden into the dirt, people with no place in society, people with no right to speak, have now audaciously lifted their heads . . . taken power into their hands. They are now running the township peasant associations."

Mao was willing to concede, however, that some peasants had overreacted. About 15 percent, he admitted, could be justly described as "riffraff." But these, he insisted, would be disciplined by the peasant associations. In any event their excesses were mild in comparison with what the peasants had suffered at the hands of the gentry:

"When the local bullies and evil gentry were at the height of their power, they killed peasants without batting an eyelid. . . . How can one say that the peasants should not now rise and shoot a few of them and bring about a small-scale reign of terror in suppressing the counter-revolutionaries?"

The Li–Ch'en clique in the CCP remained dubious of Mao's conviction that the brightest people of China ought to spend their talents joining and working with the illiterate peasantry and learn from *them* the techniques of revolution. They saw little value in Mao's insistence that the CCP should support land confiscation to assure peasant support and the provision of food supplies for the Northern Expedition.

Right-wingers in the KMT were equally opposed. They

compelled Chiang Kai-shek to complain to Stalin about the "disruptive" agitation of the peasantry by Mao and Chu. Stalin was disturbed. An outbreak of civil war between the KMT and CCP would put him in an impossible position. He had pledged his support to Chiang, yet obviously he could not support an anti-Communist crusade. He ordered Borodin to compel the CCP to pursue a more conciliatory course toward Chiang.

The CCP Central Committee obediently watered down Mao's authority to permit only limited, orderly land confiscation. Lands belonging to small landlords and parents of men in the Nationalist Army were exempted. For the moment the split between the bourgeois KMT and the revolutionary CCP was papered over. But now there was great discontent between the right and left wings of the Kuomintang.

Chiang, who had studied Mao's Hunan report, was convinced that the CCP would not be swerved from Mao's plan for a national peasant revolution to overthrow the landlord class. His apprehension was stiffened by his future father-in-law, Charlie Soong, who now acted as intermediary between Chiang and the banks, foreign interests, rich merchants, and industrialists of China. They now saw Chiang as their best hope of stopping strikes in the factories, preventing confiscation of landlords' properties, keeping servants under control, and preserving the privileges of the wealthy in China.

Soong easily persuaded Chiang that Borodin and the Communist elements in the United Front were too dangerous to tolerate any longer. Chiang's desire to marry into the powerful Soong family erased any lingering qualms.

In March, 1926, he began removing Communists from the KMT Central Executive Committee, even while the Northern Expedition continued to be a joint CCP–KMT enterprise.

Early in 1927 the left wing of the KMT sent Chou En-lai to Shanghai to organize a general strike, ostensibly plunging the city into turmoil so that Nationalist troops could take it. Charlie Soong took fright. He hurried to Chiang with an important offer from the foreign interests, banks, and rich industrialists of Shanghai. If Chiang agreed to turn on the Communists and destroy them when he took the city, Soong's combine would support him as dictator of all China.

Chiang lost little time in deciding. On the night of April 12, 1927, he sent trucks filled with his troops roaring into the heart of Shanghai. They were greeted with uproarious shouts of welcome by the striking workers. Suddenly the troops fanned out through the city, rounding up and butchering every known or even faintly suspected Communist.

Over four thousand were massacred. Professor Li Ta-chao, who had given Mao his job as assistant librarian at the University of Peking, was strangled to death by Marshal Chang Tso-lin. Chou En-lai escaped Shanghai with the help of a young officer he had befriended at the Whampoa Military Academy.

Chiang's forces smashed into and ransacked the Soviet Embassy in the city. Those Nationalist officers who had been horrified by the atrocities of the peasant uprisings in Hunan now excelled them in barbarity. A continuous line of army trucks rumbled out of Shanghai with thousands of corpses.

The general strike was crushed, and all workers forced back to their jobs. Ousted landlords hurried to reclaim their confiscated fields in KMT-held areas, extracting back rent from their wretched tenants who were now warned to have nothing further to do with "subversive" peasant associations under penalty of death. Peasants identified as Red were brutally murdered by troops.

In Moscow Stalin was stunned by Chiang's treachery.

Only the week before he had publicly praised Chiang and exchanged portraits with him. Now the Communist International was forced to denounce him as a "traitor to the people and an instrument of imperialism." On orders from Stalin, Borodin led a CCP coup, taking over the KMT government in Wuhan and expelling Chiang. Fleeing to Nanking, Chiang merely set up a rival Nationalist regime.

The Wuhan KMT government now fell into confusion, torn by arguments within the CCP faction. Seizing control, the right wing expelled Borodin and Galin, outlawed the CCP, and brought the remainder of the Wuhan regime over to Chiang.

The CCP went underground with headquarters in Canton.

Mao, disgusted by what he considered the shortsighted leadership of both the CCP and Moscow, fled to the mountains of his native Hunan to organize a new peasant army.

Gathering a tiny cadre of rural CCP leaders, he led them through the countryside whipping up peasant anger against greedy landlords, corrupt officials, and brutal police. Peasants swelled his ranks to take revenge at night with sharp sticks, spears, and pitchforks. Their fury, Mao noted in satisfaction, was like the "violence of a hurricane."

He soon had a full peasant regiment armed with rifles and ammunition captured in raids on KMT troop encampments. The underground CCP Politburo in Canton now ordered Mao to attack the cities of Hunan Province. Irked but loyal to the party, he obeyed. His crude peasant forces were no match, however, for Chiang's trained troops and were almost annihilated in a rout at Linyang. Mao himself was captured.

Led off to be beheaded, he managed to trick his guards and escape, hiding among tall, thick pond reeds until sunset ended his pursuit. A few weeks later he had rounded up about a thousand other survivors of Linyang in Kiangsi

Province. He now reorganized them as the "1st Regiment of the 1st Division of the 1st Workers' and Peasants' Revolutionary Army." Perhaps deceived by this grandiose designation, the CCP Politburo ordered Mao's ragged handful of men to attack Changsha.

Considering the mission absurd and suicidal, Mao refused. The cities, he fumed—that was all the obstinate Politburo ever thought about! In October, 1927, he led his little army instead to refuge in the impregnable Chingkangshan mountain range on the border of Hunan and Kiangsi.

Outraged, the CCP Central Committee in Canton curtly dismissed Mao from the Politburo. Word also reached him that he had been put on Chiang's death list, and KMT troops were hunting for him everywhere. Isolated from both worlds, Mao took stock of his plight to determine his future course.

The collapse of his autumn uprising in the countryside, he now felt, had been caused at least in part by his lack of military training. It was not enough merely to be a shrewd political leader. Resting in the rocky hills of Chingkangshan, he began studying the works of Sun Tzü, greatest of all Chinese military experts, to teach himself how to use guerrilla forces against superior regular armies in the field.

Learning that two bandit chiefs were operating in his remote hideout revived his boyhood admiration for the bandit heroes of his favorite novels. He invited them to join him, and they accepted, adding six hundred men to his thousand, along with 120 rifles. The CCP Politburo scornfully accused Mao of organizing "a rifle movement" instead of a revolutionary army.

"Are bandits not also outcasts of the society we fight?" he replied. "Then why should I not make common cause with them?" The bandit chiefs became regimental commanders under Mao and remained loyal to the Communist cause as long as he camped on the Chingkangshan. Afterward they reverted to banditry and were killed by peasants in the region.

Moscow was still convinced that only by taking the cities of China could the CCP win their revolution. In December, 1927, the Comintern ordered the CCP to organize a mass uprising in Canton. Squads of workers wearing red kerchiefs around their necks suddenly took control of strategic sectors of the city, burned bank buildings, and raised the Red flag over the "Canton Soviet." Chiang ordered a fierce counterattack.

Within forty-eight hours of savage fighting the Communists were reeling in defeat. Most hastily removed the red kerchiefs around their necks to avoid identification. But in the humid Canton climate the scarves had left red stains on their necks, which were instantly sliced by KMT execution squads. Among the slaughtered victims were Mao's wife, Yang K'ai-hui, one young son, and the wife of Lin Piao.

In street fighting and executions Chiang's forces killed six thousand Cantonese, stacking up and carting their bodies away in huge heaps. The blow was a crushing one to the CCP. It was small comfort to Mao, grieving on Chingkang-shan for his beloved Yang K'ai-hui and small son, that he had once more been proved right in his opposition to the Politburo strategists who saw the cities as the key to power in China.

Now Mao bitterly denounced Borodin and the Comintern as blunderers, and Li Li-san and Ch'en Tu-hsiu as "unconscious traitors." Their mistake, he vowed, had been in blindly following Marxist-Leninist theory instead of flexibly adapting it to special circumstances. "Dogma," he declared contemptuously, "is more useless than ordure."

One way had failed. He would try another.

It was only after the Chinese Communists had abandoned orthodox Bolshevik tactics that they began to win their first important victories. Mao's studies of Sun Tzü charted a new course for Red Chinese tactics.

"Fool the enemy," Sun Tzü had advised, "and wait for the right moment to profit from his confusion. . . . Avoid combat when the enemy is fresh and vigorous. Strike when he has weakened and begins to fall back. . . . The peasants can be of great use to you and serve you better than your own troops. Make them understand that they must help you in preventing the enemy from seizing their goods. . . . Love your soldiers and obtain for them everything that may lighten their task." Mao began to discover guerrilla warfare.

Chiang Kai-shek, meanwhile, had become all-powerful as China's new "strong man." Beside him now in the government palace in Nanking was a beautiful bride, Wellesley graduate Soong Mei-ling, youngest daughter of the rich Soong family. Chiang's brother-in-law was chairman of the Central Bank of China. There was no longer any doubt as to whose interests the Kuomintang party now represented.

Capturing Peking in June, 1928, Chiang began running his new Nationalist government as chairman of a one-party dictatorship. The Soong combine of domestic and international vested interests provided him with all the money and arms he needed and helped bring northern warlords under his control. Chiang was soon China's super-warlord, cloaked for camouflage in the republican mantle of Sun Yat-sen.

In desperation the CCP Executive Committee ordered Mao to undertake an all-out military campaign in southern Hunan. Since he was not specifically ordered to attack cities, he reluctantly agreed. But his forces, far too small and unready for the task in the face of huge KMT divisions, were not only easily defeated but also driven out of their base.

Fortunately for Mao, he was able to link up with the forces of Chu Teh. In the winter of 1927–1928 they managed to counterattack and retake Chingkangshan with two regiments of tattered, emaciated, poorly armed troops.

They had won, Mao reported to the CCP, only because of their total dedication to communism and their readiness to die in great numbers for their beliefs. Casualties had been heavy.

Rebuilding their base on the Hunan-Kiangsi border, Mao and Chu became close friends. They complemented each other perfectly. Mao was the calm intellectual, the philosopher, the dreamer. Chu was the warmhearted popular soldier, the practical executive. Both men shared a sense of humor, but Mao's smile was sardonic, whereas Chu's was friendly and gentle.

Although Mao had been a peasant's son and Chu the scion of a rich landowner, the bond of communism made them brothers. As their fame spread through the countryside, they were often imagined to be one man—"the famous Red general Mao-chu."

They controlled peasant associations that confiscated landlords' lands and redistributed them among the poor. Levying only the lightest taxes, their regime outlawed gambling, opium-smoking, prostitution, begging, child slavery, and compulsory marriage. Night schools were set up to reduce illiteracy. Cooperative stores marketed peasants' produce and provided them with low-cost necessities.

Such benign government under a Red Army enclave astonished peasants used to the rapacity of warlord and Nationalist troops who cut down their fruit trees, broke up their furniture for fires, slaughtered their water buffalo and hogs for food, defiled their houses, polluted their wells, plundered their shops, and outraged their wives and daughters.

It was a country saying that worthless sons were fit to be nothing but soldiers. The disciplined Red Army was different. Mao wrote and enforced a soldiers' code designed to win the hearts and minds of the civilian masses.

"Confiscate nothing from peasants," he insisted. "All

goods confiscated from landlords must be delivered promptly to headquarters. Replace all doors when you leave a house.[*] Replace any article borrowed. Be courteous and help out when you can. Be honest in all transactions with the peasants. Pay for all articles purchased. Be sanitary."

These exhortations were incorporated into a Red Army song sung daily to indoctrinate all troops. Later choruses forbade flirting with women or killing prisoners. Mao afterward claimed that during the Red Army's twelve years of war against Japan the Communists had never deliberately killed a single prisoner of war. He believed in proselytizing prisoners instead, to win them over to the Red Army.

In May, 1928, the CCP designated the forces at Chingkangshan as the Fourth Red Army, with Chu Teh as Commander in Chief and Mao as political commissar. Their forces now numbered ten thousand, but only two regiments had rifles; four were armed only with spears or sticks. Raids on KMT camps steadily increased their rifles, but at a heavy cost in men.

Chiang Kai-shek ordered his forces to retake Chingkangshan. But this time the Red Army beat off all attacks, capturing large stacks of enemy weapons. Mao wrote jubilantly:

> High in the mountains, our flags are streaming in the wind,
> Our trumpets beckon from hill to hill. . . .
> At Hwang-yang-ki our cannons thunder,
> Announcing that the enemy has fled.

Exasperated, Chiang then decided that it might be much less costly simply to buy off Mao and Chu. He sent emissaries to Chingkangshan offering them money and positions of high command in the Nationalist Army. The two Red

---

*The detachable wooden doors of Chinese houses were often used as beds by bivouacking troops.

leaders then called a mass meeting of thousands of people at their base. Introducing Chiang's envoys, Chu explained their mission.

"We could play bridge with the wives of the foreign imperialists," he told the stunned Communists, "buy concubines, sell opium, ride in automobiles, and get drunk with the gangsters of Shanghai. That is what we have been offered. We are your servants; tell us what our answer should be."

A great roar of anger boomed through the hills. "You have heard our reply," Mao told Chiang's officers quietly. "Tell your master he had better continue trying to kill Communists, because he will never be able to buy them."

Although Chu was the field commander of the Red Army, it was Mao who delivered lectures to their troops on military strategy. Guerrilla forces, Mao believed, required the ordinary soldier to have as clear a picture of goals and tactics as the Commander in Chief. One thinking, informed guerrilla fighter could outwit a squad of military robots.

Once a soldier asked him why a mobile guerrilla army like theirs needed to fight to hold on to Chingkangshan. "A base area is as necessary as the human buttocks," Mao explained. "After exhausting activity, you need it to rest on."

He made his troops understand the political issues involved in a revolutionary war—what communism was all about, and why it was worth fighting for. Every soldier was urged to be a missionary. Victory could never be theirs, Mao believed, until the peasant masses could be liberated from the old ways through reeducation by the Red Army.

In the severe winter of 1928–1929 Chiang's armies once more laid siege to Mao's base, this time encircling it with vastly superior forces. Knowing they were doomed if they tried to hold Chingkangshan, Mao and Chu led a desperate breakthrough. In fierce battles they suffered heavy losses but succeeded in getting through the blockade with 2,800 men. They set up a new base at Juichin in southern Kiangsi Province.

Li Li-san, who was now acting secretary for the CCP Central Committee, furiously denounced Mao for "un-Marxist tactics" that had almost destroyed the Fourth Red Army. He derided the "peasant mentality" that had led Mao to behave like the romantic bandit heroes of his favorite novel, *Water Margin,* instead of organizing quietly for the party.

Mao was now ordered to disperse his tattered remnants of an army into small task forces, fanning them out over the countryside to agitate the masses. He flatly refused. "The more adverse the circumstances," he replied, "the greater the need for concentrating our forces."

There was nothing the outraged CCP Central Committee could do but lump it. Stubborn, unruly, and disobedient Mao Tse-tung might be, but they needed him and his men.

Mao knew it. He was all they had.

# Chapter 5

口

# A Desperate Decision

At Juichin Mao lived in a small two-room farmhouse, sleeping on a wooden bed covered by a cotton sheet. Now thirty-six, he had married again. His new wife was Ho Tzu-chen, an attractive eighteen-year-old landlord's daughter turned revolutionary. She had first won Mao's admiration by leading a women's Communist regiment in a Nanchang uprising.

From their new base Mao and Chu campaigned constantly, making up for their small forces by mobility. Mao slept little, reading and working late every night with his writing brush, maps, documents, books, and papers. His gray uniform with large pockets was always stuffed with notes and poems.

He slung and carried his own knapsack, refusing to burden his young orderly, Chen Chang-feng, with it. In the knapsack were two blankets, a cotton sheet, an extra uniform, a tattered overcoat, a gray woolen sweater, a broken umbrella, and a small cracked eating bowl.

Often there was nothing to eat but squash. Mao composed a brave new slogan: "Down with capitalism and eat squash!" He may have meant it as wry humor, but the indoctrinated Red troops cried it aloud as an earnest of their devotion to the cause.

Mao was careful to see that officers and men alike shared

all hardships, with no privileges for anyone. "Everybody from the army commander down to the cook lives on a daily fare worth five cents, apart from grain," he reported to the Politburo now underground in Shanghai. "In the matter of pocket money, if two dimes are allotted, it is two dimes for everybody. . . . Thus the soldiers harbor no resentment."

He added, "The reason why the Red Army can sustain itself without collapse in spite of such a poor standard of material life and such incessant fighting is its practice of democracy. The officers do not beat the men; officers and men receive equal treatment; soldiers enjoy freedom of assembly and speech; cumbersome formalities and ceremonies are done away with. . . . The newly captured soldiers in particular feel that our army and the Kuomintang's army are worlds apart."

Mao was proud of the high rate of enlistment among prisoners they captured. "The soldiers feel that they are not fighting for somebody else," he pointed out, "but for themselves and for the people. . . . The fact that the same soldier who was not brave in the enemy army yesterday becomes very brave in the Red Army today shows precisely the impact of democracy."

Democracy did not mean to Mao rule by majority but the rule of equal treatment for all by honest leaders. That was a far more just system, he believed, than a western-style political democracy where popular opinion was manipulated by press lords, so that a majority of the people were misled into voting for measures the capitalists wanted.

Enjoying the rugged life he lived, Mao felt increasing contempt for his city-bound comrades of the CCP Central Committee. "Some people," he wrote acidly, "lack the patience to carry on arduous struggles together with the masses, and only want to go to the big cities to eat and drink to their hearts' content."

He inspired his troops with an equally stoic pride in their

hardships. When they had no cannon, which was most of the time, they made them out of hollow tree trunks reinforced with iron bands. When they had too few rifles, they fought with spears and bows and arrows. When they had no food, they attacked Nationalist villages at night to get it. They endured vermin until the weather was warm enough to let them strip and boil their ragged clothes. When they had no shoes, they bound their feet in rags.

Their rigors left them skeleton-thin. But they endured.

When food was available, Mao lived mostly on rice "sandwiches"—two layers of rice with cooked vegetables between. Once he didn't quite finish his bowlful, and Chen dumped the leavings. Mao tongue-lashed him for extravagance.

"There is a struggle for every grain of rice that the people grow," he reproached Chen. "In future you mustn't throw away what I leave. Keep it for my next meal." When war booty was captured, Mao never kept anything for himself, distributing it instead among his subordinates or sending it to wounded troops in his field hospital.

In June, 1930, Li Li-san once more convinced the CCP Central Committee that all-out attacks on the major cities of south-central China would bring about worker uprisings that would topple Chiang Kai-shek. Mao and Chu reluctantly obeyed. The Red Army fought into Changsha and captured it, then advanced on Nanchang. But after bitter battles with vastly superior forces they were forced to retreat.

The Nationalists then swiftly overran Changsha, sweeping up thousands of Chinese who had cooperated with the Red Army during the ten days it had held the city. Among those seized and beheaded was Mao's sister, Mao Tse-hung.

Mao had had enough. At a December, 1930, conference in Lushan, he demanded the ouster of Li Li-san as a dangerous fool whose reckless decisions were wrecking the Red

Army. This time he was supported by Chou En-lai. Li Li-san was rebuked by the Central Committee, then exiled to Moscow to expiate his costly tactical mistakes. Mao was elected Chairman of the Workers' and Peasants' Revolutionary Committee.

During the next three years Chiang Kai-shek launched four major but inconclusive campaigns to surround Mao's base at Juichin and strangle it. The first "Encirclement and Annihilation Campaign" threw one hundred thousand KMT troops against a Red Army that Mao and Chu had built back up to forty thousand.

By skillful maneuvering, Mao enticed individual enemy battalions into ambushes where they were slaughtered piecemeal by hidden concentrations of larger Red Army forces. Peasants everywhere served as Mao's eyes, ears, and supply depots. Their information led to the capture of the enemy commanding general. Mao turned him over to the peasants, who tried and executed him for crimes against civilians.

A frustrated Chiang Kai-shek organized his Second Campaign against Mao, this time sending two hundred thousand men against a Red Army reduced by battle to thirty thousand. Using the same shrewd tactics, Mao not only drove off the bewildered Nationalists but also captured twenty thousand of their rifles.

Beside himself with rage, Chiang Kai-shek took personal command of the Third Campaign, leading three hundred thousand crack troops against the Red base at Juichin. This time the Nationalists advanced swiftly in force without stopping to rest or consolidate gains. Racing to overtake the fleet Red Army, Chiang sought to smother it in one giant tidal wave of men.

Mao let the Nationalists penetrate deep inside the base area. Then he slipped his forces around their flanks and made hit-and-run night attacks against the weakest KMT units at Chiang's rear. Confused, exhausted, and demoralized, the enemy milled around blindly in vain search of the elusive Red Army, more often firing at each other than at Communists.

And under cover of darkness, chuckling in contempt, Mao and Chu robbed them of extensive war matériel. Chiang was finally forced to withdraw, his Third Campaign of Annihilation a humiliating failure. One of his generals complained bitterly of the peasants' refusal to cooperate with the KMT forces.

"Everywhere the National Army gropes in the dark," he lamented, "while the Red Army moves freely in broad daylight."

Mao later told André Malraux, "It is a question of having more men or more courage in the place where you give battle. An occasional defeat is inevitable; you simply need to have more victories than defeats."

On September 18, 1931, as Chiang was vainly trying to stamp out the Red Army, Tokyo launched an attack on Manchuria. Sweeping aside Chiang's warlords, the Japanese were able to conquer the province in less than six months. Setting up a puppet government, they renamed the province Manchukuo.

Their grab of half a million square miles infuriated all Chinese. From the underground in Shanghai the CCP Central Committee declared war on the Japanese. The Kuomintang vainly sought to suppress all news about Manchuria. Chiang did not want to be pressured by public opinion into giving up his campaign against the Communists to fight the Japanese.

By now Mao had clearly established himself as the most eminent and effective force in the Communist party. He had been proven right consistently; the Li Li-san faction had been discredited. At Mao's insistence the CCP Central Committee now left Shanghai—an abandonment of the city at last—to establish a new headquarters at the base in Jui-chin.

Now a First Congress of Chinese Soviets was convened to set up a rival national government to Chiang's—the Chinese Soviet Republic. Mao Tse-tung was elected its first Chairman, and Chu Teh renamed Commander in Chief of the Red Army. In an acceptance speech Mao estimated that they now had the support of about thirty million Chinese under their jurisdiction, half this number living in and around Kiangsi Province in southeastern China.

Mao was now preeminent in the CCP, yet his powers were not unlimited. Final authority still rested in the hands of the sixty-three-member Central Committee. Many of these leaders, foreign-trained and Moscow-oriented, still had grave reservations about Mao's "guerrillaism"—"playing bandit" in the countryside against Chiang's regulars instead of developing in secret a mass uprising against the Nationalist government.

To curb Mao's military authority, they appointed Chou En-lai political commissar over the Red Army in Mao's place. Chou could be depended upon not to allow any faction in the CCP to go to extremes that might split the party. Mao's opponents were still far from convinced that his beloved peasantry was a suitable substitute for Marx's proletariat.

In 1932 the Japanese attacked and took Shanghai, forcing Chiang's troops to retreat to Fukien Province. Chiang made abject peace overtures to Tokyo, negotiating with the Japanese for a pact that would let them do pretty much as they pleased in return for letting him concentrate on fighting the Communists. Wasn't that in their interests, too?

Resuming his offensive against the Red Army, Chiang offered bribes to the peasants of Kiangsi for the capture of Red Army officers and noncommissioned officers. A price of $250,000 each in silver—raised from $100,000—was now set on the severed heads of Mao Tse-tung and Chu Teh.

Chiang was answered by sunrise in KMT-occupied towns, which revealed nighttime additions to wall posters. They read: "Brothers in the White Armies! For whom are you fighting and why? Your pay goes into the pockets of your officers. You are mercenaries of oppressors and imperialists. The poor should not attack the poor!" By the beginning of 1932 over two hundred thousand KMT troops had deserted to the Red Army.

"The Reds have made platoons of our battalions," lamented the chief of staff of one of Chiang's brigades. "And of the platoons, there is nothing left but corpses!"

Wherever Chiang's troops struck in force, the Red Army melted away into forests, abandoning villages impossible to defend. They would reappear suddenly where least expected, cutting rear echelons to pieces. Mao's chief asset in this kind of guerrilla warfare was plenty of space filled with mountains and forests, each of which had a hidden maze of trails. Local Reds knew these trails well and guided their comrades along them to withdraw or make surprise attacks.

In the winter of 1932–1933, however, impatient members of the CCP Central Committee challenged Mao's defensive strategy. The time had come, they insisted, for a head-on clash with Chiang's forces to topple the Kuomintang. Besides, they pointed out, what sort of Soviet Republic was it that could not prevent the enemy from penetrating its territory? Didn't they have an obligation to protect their people?

"We must not have illusions about a war of advance without any retreats," Mao warned in reply, "or take alarm at any temporary fluidity of our Soviet territory. . . . It is only out of today's fluid way of life that tomorrow we can secure relative stability."

His views were denounced as those of a "military romanticist" who prolonged war by regarding it as the supreme adventure and test of human courage. Mao's shortcoming was "too narrowly Chinese a view of revolution," instead of relating it to a constantly changing world situation. His rivals sought to coordinate Chinese moves with Moscow policy as Franklin D. Roosevelt became the new American President and Adolf Hitler was named Chancellor of Nazi Germany.

Chiang Kai-shek began his Fourth Encirclement Campaign against Juichin in the winter of 1932–1933. The CCP Central Committee directed the Red Army to repel the Nationalists with head-on clashes. Not expecting this change in strategy, Chiang lost thirteen thousand men in a single battle. Mao's rivals were jubilant, and he was forced to acknowledge the success of their tactics. He celebrated the victory in rhyme:

> Red, orange, yellow, green, blue indigo, violet—
> Who is dancing in the sky, whirling this ribbon of color?
> . . . A desperate battle raged here once.
> Bullet holes pit the walls of the village.
> They are an adornment,
> And today the hills seem yet more fair.

Nevertheless he remained dubious of the long-range wisdom of conventional warfare in the face of a numerically superior, well-trained, well-armed enemy. His views were soon validated by Chiang's importation of a German military adviser, General von Falkenhausen, who changed Nationalist tactics for a Fifth Encirclement Campaign that began in October, 1933.

Falkenhausen put a million KMT troops, half led by Chiang himself, in an iron ring around Kiangsi that was gradually squeezed tighter and tighter. It was a massive blockade intended to starve the Red Army and the population they controlled into submission. An air force of four hundred bombers, reinforced by artillery, pounded them mercilessly.

*This* time, Chiang assured the Soong syndicate, Mao and his comrades were safely caged, unable to escape. A ring of blockhouses linked by barbed wire barred every path of flight. The choking iron collar tightened gradually, isolating Red Army units into thickets and gullies where they could be mopped up. By the summer of 1934 shortages of food, arms, and ammunition had made Mao's situation desperate.

Enemy planes roared overhead, dropping bombs and strafing indiscriminately all hours of the day. Mao, from headquarters in a hillside Buddhist temple, exchanged tactical dispatches with Chou En-lai. The Red Army, Mao complained, was floundering in a net like trapped fish.

"This is really the worst and most stupid way to fight," he protested. Trying to puzzle a way out of the dilemma, he slept little, neglected his meals, and studied battle reports and marked maps far into the night. He lost weight and grew haggard. When his worried orderly protested, he promised Chen gently, "I'll take a rest as soon as I've finished these documents. Will that be all right?" The plight of the Red Army kept him sleepless, though.

He was now sure of only one thing: Positional defense against a stronger enemy was catastrophic. The Red Army's only hope of survival now lay in breaking out of the steel trap. True, they had held out in Kiangsi for seven years. But Mao knew that further attempts at resistance would be fatal.

One way or another the entire Chinese Communist Republic and its armed forces would have to smash through Chiang's deadly iron ring and escape to some distant, secure base. But how? Where?

The surrounding plains and seacoast were controlled by Chiang. If the Reds were to survive, it could only be by undertaking an enormous evasive flight north through awesome mountain paths and gorges where no Chinese had ever dared travel before. And to escape, they would have to throw off blockaders and pursuers by winding around and doubling back on their own trail like a gigantic serpent, marching six useless miles for every real one they put behind them.

Mao discussed these ideas with Chu Teh. Chu agreed that their casualties were bound to be terrible. But if they stayed in Kiangsi, the whole Communist nation would be wiped out to the last man. Mao's plan offered the only hope of preserving the chance for a future Socialist China.

In January, 1934, at the Second All-China Soviet Congress, Mao presented his plan, and Chu urged its acceptance. The CCP Central Committee was forced to agree that it offered the best chance of survival. Secret preparations began for the evacuation of Juichin's 100,000 troops and those civilians who chose to risk breaking out with them.

A Red Army vanguard probing weak points in Chiang's blockade met with disaster. Falkenhausen's blockhouses cut it to pieces. One column led by Lin Piao managed to get through but only after suffering severe losses.

The die, nevertheless, was cast. On October 16, 1934, the Red Army slipped out of Juichin under cover of night, accompanied by thousands of civilians, including thirty-five women and a few children. Diversionary attacks by suicide squads of partisan volunteers busied Nationalist troops in another direction. It was almost forty-eight hours before Chiang's forces discovered the Red Army's exodus through forest trails.

So began an epic journey often compared to Hannibal's crossing of the Alps. In over a year of relentless marching through snowcapped mountains, plunging gorges, vast deserts, and swamplands, the First Front Army under Mao Tse-tung covered on foot the distance of 7,500 agonizing miles.

His ultimate destination was unknown. "We had no exact plans," he admitted later. His primary objective was escape from the powerful Nationalist armies surrounding them, outnumbering them twenty to one, so that they might live to fight another day. But they were kept under fierce attack, on the ground and from the air, for their whole year of flight.

When the "Long March" began, the CCP Central Committee was in supreme command. The Red Army was under the tactical command of Chu Teh with Chou En-lai as political commissar. Mao and Lin Piao each led advance columns of troops wearing hats topped by leaf camouflage and carrying red-tasseled pikes.

In long, winding columns they marched southwest to probe weak spots in Falkenhausen's fire wall. During the first month, harassed by air attacks, the marchers fought nine battles to break through four lines of blockhouses and 110 regiments. When they smashed through the third enemy cordon, Chiang Kai-shek dispatched four hundred thousand troops to pursue and intercept them along the Hsiangkiang River.

Knowing they were in a race against time, Mao urged the Politburo to dump the sewing machines, printing presses, gold and silver bullion, and other heavy impedimenta that was slowing down the columns. His advice was rejected. Finding Chiang's forces wheeling into position between the Red Army and the Hsiangkiang, the Politburo ordered a head-on attack.

The Red Army succeeded in breaking through and crossing the river, but at the terrible cost of a full third of their forces. Bitter criticism was leveled at the Politburo for failing to heed Mao. Now, belatedly, the Politburo ordered the dumping of all encumbrances except military equipment and a few field printing presses.

Chiang, meanwhile, ordered his commanders, warlords,

and military governors in regions through which the Red Army had to pass to cut bridges, sink junks, reinforce garrisons, and keep the marchers under bombardment day and night. Chu Teh wanted to keep pressing ahead as speedily as possible. But Mao now urged night marches only, hiding by day, as long as they were within range of Chiang's air force. He pointed out that they must now avoid any more pitched battles at all costs. The way to fight free was to isolate the fingers of the Kuomintang forces probing everywhere for them and chop off one at a time, persistently.

Mao's advice prevailed. The Red Army marched nights and slept mornings. In the afternoon they would plait straw sandals, clean rifles, and prepare to move out. A bugle call summoned them to supper. At a second call they fell in for a daily orientation talk by their unit political instructor. A third blast started the night march.

Heeding Mao, Chu Teh now constantly changed their direction to confuse and baffle the Nationalists. Often they took a whole night crossing one mountain, marching in crowded columns along narrow, winding alpine paths. They could not shake off their pursuers for long, however, because enemy troops could travel swiftly along the easier regular roads.

In late December Mao's advance column blazed a snowy trail to the Wukiang River in central Kweichow. Seeking to cross it to hold the opposite bank for the main Red Army against enemy patrols, Mao was warned by local peasants that boats couldn't navigate the turbulent currents.

Deciding to chance it with bamboo rafts, he ordered his men to construct them. For three days they fought vainly to pole through the Wukiang's violent waves, buffeted by icy winds. When two rafts managed to get through the worst of the rapids, they were suddenly turned back by machine-gun fire from enemy cliff posts.

Undiscouraged, Mao then waited for nightfall and asked

for volunteers to join him in crossing by starlight. On the night of January 2, 1935, he led the way in the first raft with four men. Miraculously, they poled silently and safely to the opposite shore. To keep warm in the freezing night while waiting for reinforcements, they huddled together beneath the cliff with the machine-gun posts. They could hear the enemy's voices and laughter, loud and confident.

The night wore on. No more rafts landed.

"Don't worry," Mao whispered to his men. "Our troops will come. If not tonight, tomorrow. Don't worry!"

# Chapter 6

# The Long March

*"May you live in the most interesting of times."*
—Ancient Chinese curse

Shortly before dawn three more rafts managed to make it across the river. Mao found an unguarded route to the top of the cliff. He and his men then attacked the gun posts with grenades and tommy-guns, silencing them. A rope was then stretched across the Wukiang, and the main body of the Red Army had no further difficulty crossing the river in rafts.

Next day the marchers fought through villages en route to the enemy stronghold at Tsunyi. They took many prisoners, who were astonished by their courteous treatment.

"Our officers told us," one Nationalist soldier reported, "that you were all horrible creatures who indulged in orgies of killing and burning houses. They said if we fell into your hands, you'd gouge out our eyeballs and disembowel us. We had no idea that you were decent people!"

One impressed captured commander agreed to lead Red Army troops, disguised in enemy uniforms, to Tsunyi, pretending they were remnants of his battalion returning to the city. The ruse worked, and the wall-gates were opened. As the Red Army vangaurd entered the city, one KMT sentry said, "I hear the Communist bandits are advancing pretty fast. Are they across the Wukiang yet?"

"Oh, yes," nodded one Red Army man in a Nationalist uniform. "In fact, hands up, please."

Pointing rifles at the KMT guard detachment, the Communists forced them back from the gates as the rest of the Red Army materialized from the darkness. Red buglers sounded a charge, and Mao's forces raced into the city. Sleeping Nationalist troops had barely time to get out of their barracks and flee undressed out the north gate.

In the morning the people of Tsunyi lined the streets to cheer their liberators and express their joy with firecrackers. Mao was concerned, however. By this time the Workers' and Peasants' Red Army had lost fully 60 percent of its men, mostly due to the CCP Politburo's inept leadership.

At a special Politburo conference in Tsunyi he denounced two fundamental mistakes constantly made in the handling of the main forces of the Red Army—headlong flight and open clashes with Chiang's troops to break through. They should always use guerrilla tactics, he insisted, turning and twisting, advancing and retreating, to catch the enemy by surprise. Chiang's forces had to be kept on the defensive at all times, never knowing whether to retreat, advance, or dig in.

"Enemy advances, we retreat," Mao explained. "Enemy halts, we harass. Enemy tires, we attack. Enemy retreats, we pursue. In territory which favors us, we adopt the policy of advancing in a series of waves. When pursued by a powerful enemy in territory favorable to them, we adopt the policy of circling around in a whirling motion."

He proposed a new slogan to change the spirit of the Long March from one of flight to fight: "Go north to fight the Japanese!" This would also brand Chiang a traitor for seeking to stop them and would encourage recruitment.

Mao's ideas carried the day. Not only was he named secretary of the CCP Central Committee, but a new post—Chairman of the Politburo—was also created to give him absolute powers of decision over the Long March.

Mao's new strategy went into effect immediately. In one month, February, 1935, the inspirited First Front Army wiped out four enemy divisions, its first great victory since the Long March had begun. Great praise was heaped on Mao for once more proving right. His views were now listened to with a respectful deference that stroked his vanity.

After a two-week rest at Tsunyi word reached Mao that Nationalist troops were advancing against them from the south. Moving his columns out, he left small forces behind to fight a delaying action. Among them was his brother Mao Tse-t'an, who was killed in battle shortly afterward.

Winding his way deviously through Kweichow Province, Mao threw his pursuers off the track by sending a small unit conspicuously east while leading the main force secretly west through mountain trails. When Chiang's troops massed in a logical area to strike a crushing blow, they would find themselves attacked suddenly from the rear or flanks. Hastily re-forming their ranks, they would counter-attack empty space while the Red Army was serenely slipping away elsewhere.

The enemy was compelled to rearrange troop formations constantly with each new Communist maneuver dictated by Mao's military cunning. He lured KMT forces wherever he wanted them by feints that drew them into traps or took them out of his path. His adroit tactics gave the Red Army ample opportunity to rest at times of their own choosing. Mao's assiduous self-study of Sun Tzü on the Chingkang-shan was now rewarding the Red Army far more gener-ously than Chiang's formal studies in Moscow and his military academy at Whampoa were helping the National-ists.

Wherever Mao led, oppressed peasants were liberated, government records of "malcontents" and property deeds were burned, and sacks of rice, salt, and money were distributed among the people. The Red Army opened prisons, freeing naked and half-starved tax delinquents who had been tortured and jailed in irons for a dozen years and more. The released victims were sympathetically fed, clothed, and doctored.

It was hardly surprising that in areas the Red Army passed through, they were showered with gifts of food, wine, shoes, and cloth. Recruits rushed to join their ranks.

Mao sought to enforce strict rules of sanitation on his wandering army, but mosquito-borne malaria took its toll. Mao and his orderly both fell ill. Mao cared for Chen himself, taking over the storm lantern from the youth on night marches in the rain, so that the violently trembling Chen would not fall. Despite his own attacks, he wrote reassuring letters home to Chen's parents, mailed by peasants.

"Chairman," Chen said, weeping, "I am supposed to take care of you, and instead you are taking care of me!"

Hard at their heels pressed Chiang's crack army and airforce units while in front of them Chiang's provincial warlords set up armed blockades at natural barriers. "For twelve months we were under daily reconnaissance and bombing from the air by scores of planes," Mao wrote later. "We were encircled, pursued, obstructed and intercepted on the ground by a big force of several hundred thousand men. We encountered untold difficulties and great obstacles on the way. . . . Has there ever been in history a long march like ours? No, never. The Long March . . . proclaims to the world that the Red Army is an army of heroes."

More and more Mao began to see himself as a man of destiny. Despite death all around him, he had been miraculously spared. Why—if not because a mysterious fate had decreed him to be the Chinese Moses? He grew increasingly indifferent about his personal safety. What would be, would be.

Secure in his fatalism, he frequently turned his face away from war to contemplate the beauty and grandeur of the lands he and his men fought through. Often the morning bugles found him already awake, busily writing poetry to celebrate both his love of the outdoors and his cause:

Cold is the west wind,
And the cry of wild geese is heard in the frosty air of the morning moonlight.
In the morning moonlight
The clatter of horses' hooves rings sharp,
And the bugle's note is muted.
The mountain pass before us is awesome, but it is not unconquerable.
This very day with one great step we shall pass its sea-blue peaks.

Ironically sensitive to beauty in the midst of battle, he would write, "On the battlefield yellow flowers are singularly fragrant," and "the landscape is strangely charming." Echoing the romantic bandit heroes of the novels he had loved as a youth, he would muse:

Narrow pathways, silent forests, delicate mosses,
Where will our footsteps lead us today?
The red flag unfolds like a sun in the wind. . . .
Day will be dawning in the east.
Let no one say that we have begun to march too soon.
Man does not grow old walking through greening hills.

The poet in Mao never superseded the revolutionary, though. More and more the Long March became for him not merely an escape from Chiang's powerful forces, but a propaganda crusade to convert the Chinese masses to communism. He even organized an "agit-prop" road show that gave anticapitalist, anti-Japanese performances in villages after a hard day's march.

"Without the Long March," he asked, "how could the broad masses have known so quickly that there are such great ideas in the world as are upheld by the Red Army? The Long March is also a seeding-machine. It has sown many seeds in eleven provinces, which will sprout, grow leaves, blossom into flowers, bear fruit and yield a harvest in the future."

There was little doubt that the peasants supported Mao. "They soon realized that the Red Army was their own," he told André Malraux. "Almost everywhere it had a friendly reception. It helped the peasants, especially at harvest time. They saw that there was no privileged class among us. They saw that we all ate the same food and wore the same clothes. The soldiers were free to meet and free to talk. . . . The officers did not have the right to strike the men or to insult them. . . . In the liberated areas, life was less terrible."

Aware that the masses were turning against him, Chiang sought to frighten the peasantry by spreading rumors that the Reds buried prisoners and peasants alive and "communized wives and property." But nothing worked more in Mao's favor than the spontaneous gossip to the effect that Red Army recruits seemed to enjoy their lives with Mao far more than they had in their home villages and were even being taught to read and write as they marched north.

The Red Army's literacy school was a novel one. Women with the march wore placards inscribed with Chinese characters tied to their backs. Day after day, mile by mile, these characters engraved themselves on the minds of soldiers who followed behind until they had memorized enough characters to permit them to read.

More personal tragedy struck Mao. Once when they were under air attack his wife, Ho Tzu-chen, now heavy with child, was unable to move swiftly enough. Low-flying dive bombers roared overhead, and she fell with twenty pieces of shrapnel in her body. She lived only because Mao himself doctored her wounds with herbal medicines.

Because Ho could now no longer look after their two

small children, Mao took them to a nearby mountain hovel and left them with a peasant family for safekeeping. "We shall never see them again!" Ho wept miserably.

Nor did they, even though years later Mao instituted a prolonged search for them. Whenever Ho grew sad about their loss, Mao would sigh philosophically, "One must not mourn two seeds in a forest of seven hundred million trees."

During the Long March he took over 150,000 prisoners, holding them four or five days to let them see for themselves what the Red Army was really like. Those who then wished to leave were allowed to do so and were even given a cordial farewell ceremony. Many preferred to stay and fight with the Red Army. Most others avoided returning to their old units, or they weakened Nationalist fighting spirit by spreading pro-Mao reports.

In April, 1935, Mao led an advance echelon across the Golden Sand (Yangtze) River on the Szechwan-Yunnan border. Rowing across with his orderly, he could barely stay awake, not having slept for days. Curling up on the Yunnan shore under an oilcloth in a dripping cave, he sought forty winks. He rose to find that Chen had prepared a bowl of hot rice for him but no board or flat stone for him to write on.

"Food or drink are trifles at a time like this," Mao reproached. "Only work is important! Don't you realize our comrades are waiting to cross the river? It's a matter of thirty thousand lives—not hot rice for a military leader!"

It took nine days and nine nights for the Red Army to cross the churning river that roared like a cloudburst through a sheer, mile-high mountain gorge. Strung out for mile upon mile, the troops crossed first, followed by civilians.

Local peasants in Yunnan cautioned Mao against the aboriginal Lolos of the forest regions through which the

Red Army had to pass. "They are savages who hate the Chinese people," he was warned, "and love to fight." Mao instructed his troops to assure the Lolos that they were not brutal Chinese like the Nationalists but respected all tribal peoples and considered them brothers.

One Red commander reported difficulty because his men couldn't understand Lolo speech. "It's as if we were in a foreign country," he complained.

Mao nodded. "That's not surprising. You know how big our country is. You, a Kiangsi man, can't even understand what I, a Hunan man, say. So how can you hope to understand the Lolos? But we must communicate with them by kindness."

The Lolos tested Mao's sincerity by demanding weapons to use against the Nationalists. Chu Teh was dubious about the wisdom of arming them. But Mao pointed out that showing obvious distrust was even riskier. Armed, the gratified Lolos then guided them through secret forest paths so secluded that the Nanking air force lost all trace of them.

Chiang knew, however, that the Red Army had to cross the Tatu River, which ran through a towering mountain gorge deeper than the Yangtze. A century earlier the rebel army of a Taiping prince had been trapped in this gorge by the forces of Manchu warlords, and all one hundred thousand men had been killed.

Chiang counted on similarly exterminating the Red Army at the Tatu. The Long March, he grimly assured the Soongs, would shortly become the Communists' funeral march.

En route to the Tatu, Mao, who now had a horse, insisted on dismounting and walking with his men. He turned the horse over to a wounded Red Army man who protested, "Comrade Mao, I am just a common soldier and my death would be of no importance. But I am on horseback and you on foot. We need you too much to think of our own condition. Please, mount!"

Mao refused. "You will not die, comrade," he promised, "nor shall I. We will live, we will fight, we will think together until victory. Why else are we Communists?"

Reaching Anshunch'ang at the Tatu, Mao managed to capture three small Nationalist boats for their crossing. But the river was so turbulent and dangerous with spring floods pouring down the mountains that it took two hours for a single passage. At that rate the crossing would take weeks.

Several hundred thousand KMT troops were hot on their heels. Worse, the Red Army had already been located by Chiang's dive bombers, who swooped over the gorge upsetting one boat with a near miss. The two others hastily turned back.

Conferring with a Lolo guide, Mao learned that there was one other possible place to cross the Tatu—a suspension bridge at Lutingch'iao, sixty miles west. A narrow trail wound there through the river gorge.

At nightfall Mao ordered all pack animals left behind as he prepared to lead the Red Army along the trail. One Red commander protested that most of the men were now barefoot; the rocks of the gorge would cut their feet to pieces. Mao calmly took off his own threadbare sandals and threw them into the river. Then he led the way by torchlight.

The weird procession through the gorge was lit by ten thousand eerie yellow flames. It moved with exasperating slowness along slippery, razor-sharp rocks. At times the narrow trail ran high above the raging stream. Then without warning it would plunge precipitously to the level of the race.

Sometimes they had to fight through deep mud. Bones chilled in the icy damp of the night; exhausted men collapsed and fell into the torrents. Marchers behind stared sadly for a moment, then closed ranks. Now and then a woman or child slipped on the mossy rocks, plunging into the boiling depths with a terrified scream.

The march along the gorge wall seemed like a nightmare without end. Mao's political cadres urged the weary column forward, exhorting the marchers not to take the easy way and die, but to struggle on with Mao, who was setting them an example at the head of the procession.

The barefoot leader had given away his coat to a wounded soldier, indifferent to the damp drizzle that soaked him now in the biting night wind. As lesser men around him succumbed and fell, Mao was sustained by the body he had toughened by a lifetime of mountaineering and icy river swims.

On the second day in the gorge Mao trained field glasses to the north and saw Nationalist troops racing from the northeast toward Lutingch'iao. Mao quickened his pace and signaled the weary column behind him to hurry. Every second counted in beating the KMT forces to the bridge.

Rain pelted them mercilessly. Roaring torrents rushed down the mountain gullies, spray making the twisting path alongside the gorge as slippery as oil. Mao and his men lurched, half-fell, and stumbled forward. Some men were now dozing on their feet. A soldier who halted would be pushed awake by the man behind him.

On Mao's orders the troops unwound their puttees and used them as wrist grips to tie themselves together in a long chain, helping each other along safely. Seething below, like an eager monster waiting for victims, the Tatu sent huge white waves dashing against giant boulders. No man who fell into the boiling currents could or did survive. That night the torches of the Red Army on one side of the river and those of racing KMT troops on the other crimsoned the waters of the Tatu.

Mao's forces were first to reach Lutingch'iao, but his jaw fell at the sight of the bridge. Nine large iron chains, each over three hundred feet long with links as thick as rice bowls, dipped over the steep chasm from blockhouses on both sides.

Planks had originally been laid across the chains, but almost all had been taken up by the enemy on the other side, where the city of Luting stood. Two enemy regiments were dug into strong fortifications built along the cliff slope with machine-gun and mortar emplacements facing the bridge.

A guard's mocking shout floated across the river. "Let's see you *fly* over, comrades!"

# Chapter 7

# Through Mountain Blizzards and Swamp Fog

The Red Army's only hope of crossing the bridge was to win control of the north end first, pin down enemy fire, and capture the planks to re-lay on the chains—but how? Conferring with Chu Teh, Mao suggested that a suicide squad might be able to cross hand over hand, hanging from the chains with grenades in their pockets and tommy-guns slung on their backs. Chu agreed that it was their only hope and volunteered to lead the squad.

"No, I will," Mao replied. "I would not ask any man to do what I am not willing to do myself."

When the plan was explained to an advance Red echelon, though, hundreds of men volunteered and refused to consent to the risk of losing either Mao or Chu unnecessarily. An assault party of twenty-two muscular men was selected, who would be followed by a company of plank-layers.

The attack began at 4 P.M. As regiment buglers sounded a spirited charge, Red machine guns opened fire on enemy emplacements across the river. Then one by one the volunteers swung out over the boiling torrents of the Tatu on the nine swaying chains in the face of intense Nationalist fire.

Roaring winds in the gorge tore first one, then a second soldier from desperate grips on the wet links, hurling them to destruction. Others on the bellying chains were blown at grotesque angles, like puppets dangling from giant strings. Hand over hand, swinging their bodies, they heaved their way rhythmically forward toward the north bank. Those hit by enemy fire plummeted into the fierce rapids and disappeared.

A few oil-soaked planks had been left on the north side of the chains. As the first Red soldiers reached them, a hurled enemy torch set them ablaze. Dashing through the fire barrier, members of the assault squad flung hand grenades at machine-gun posts outside Luting's west gate. One man, hurled back by a stitch of enemy bullets, fell into the raging waters with his uniform ablaze like a falling red star.

The grenades silenced the machine guns, however, and in a matter of seconds other Red soldiers were pouring through the curtain of flame, weapons firing. Some seized the stacked planks on the north shore and began passing them swiftly back to be laid on the chains, working backward toward the south shore. The assault squad kept the KMT forces tied down until the Red Army began crossing the bridge at top speed.

All members of the heroic twenty-two-man assault team were killed, but Red forces smashed their way into Luting and overpowered enemy regiments in a two-hour battle. Meanwhile the full force of the Red Army poured across the Tatu as Chiang's dive bombers vainly sought to knock out the swaying bridge. The KMT force that had been racing Mao to Luting along the north shore arrived woefully late and turned away.

Chiang's effort to bottle up and destroy the Red Army in the gorge before it could escape into Szechwan Province had failed. Mao's ingenious generalship at the Tatu had opened the way to the north and the snowy mountains of Tibet. His stock had never been higher among his followers, who now acclaimed him as a military genius.

Even worse ordeals were to come, though. Another two thousand miles of marching, across seven giant mountain ranges, lay ahead before they could reach safety. Mao's goal was now Shensi, a sparsely populated far-north province that had fallen under provincial Communist control. The marchers' journey took them through desolate regions inhabited only by some warrior tribes who held the mountain passes. They suffered constantly from bitter cold and little food.

By June, 1935, they managed to reach the foot of the sixteen-thousand-foot Tahsueh (Great Snow) Mountains, which superstitious local people called the Fairy Mountains because "only spirit creatures can fly over Ma An-shan Pass." Mao advised his followers to fortify themselves against freezing cold by collecting and chewing ginger, as he did.

On June 1, the 230th day of the Long March, the long Red column wound slowly up the towering snow-covered peak. After twenty minutes marchers began to flounder in snowdrifts. Some fell through into crevasses and had to be rescued.

The rare atmosphere of the freezing altitudes proved too much for many exhausted, thinly clad marchers from the south. Hundreds perished from exposure, dying silently in the all-effacing snow. Men who stopped to rest, huddling together for warmth, never got up again. Gunners bent under the weight of mortar barrels found every step utter agony.

Mao kept slipping back as he climbed, helped by men around him and helping them. His uniform was as paper-thin as theirs, his thin gray trousers and black cotton shoes perpetually soaked. When Chen sought to support him, he waved his young orderly away. "No," he panted, "you're just as weary as I am."

Halfway up the mountain thick dark clouds descended

from the ten-thousand-foot top of the pass, bearing swirling gusts of new snow. Then knifelike winds began pelting them with hailstones. One group around Mao turned their backs and sheltered beneath an oilskin sheet.

"Hold on, comrades!" Mao shouted above the raging storm. "Don't give up! Keep pushing on! We mustn't stop!"

His propaganda teams exhorted the climbers to press on through the blizzard. Plowing forward himself, Mao found his heart racing, his breath difficult to catch. Local peasants had warned, "Don't talk or laugh as you approach the pass, or the god of the mountain will choke you to death!"

The first climbers who reached the summit collapsed in groups of three to five, staring in awe at the sunlit vista above the clouds, through which terrifying alps pierced as far as the eye could see. They begged Mao to let them rest.

"Not here, comrades," he urged. "The air is too rarefied. Come, make one final effort, and we shall soon link up with the Fourth Front Army."

As they slipped down the shadowed side of the Great Snow Mountain, the cold grew more intense and numbing. Chen collapsed. Mao picked him up and helped him along until the orderly recovered halfway down the mountain.

On the 251st day Mao himself began to stagger, sick with a burning fever. Only half-conscious, he had to be carried for several days on a stretcher.

At last, on June 12, 1935, Mao and forty-five thousand weary, ragged survivors stumbled into Mouking, where the Fourth Front Army under Chang Kuo-t'ao was waiting to link up with Mao's First. Mao had known Chang Kuo-t'ao at Peking University when he worked there as a library assistant.

A cofounder of the CCP like Mao, Chang had been among those critical of Mao's high regard for the peasantry. As his former superior in the party, Chang had scoffed, "All your peasants care about is having a true Son of Heaven to rule them and a bumper crop." Now Mao was the leader of the CCP, however, and Chang could no longer dismiss his views. In Mouking the skeleton-thin survivors, safe at last for a while, collapsed for an almost solid month of sleep and rest.

On August 1, 1935, Mao issued an "Appeal to Fellow-Countrymen for Resistance to Japan and National Salvation." It called for an end to the civil war between Nationalists and Communists and a United Front against the invaders.

Chiang Kai-shek, however, was telling the Chinese people, "If we do not wait for the opportune moment but start war rashly and prematurely, the result will be only defeat and ruin. Not ten days but three days would suffice for the Japanese to seize all the strategic points on the coast or along the rivers. In fact, they could seize any place they wanted." Chiang vastly preferred to keep fighting the enemy he regarded a far greater menace—Mao Tse-tung.

Mao expected Chang Kuo-t'ao to add the Fourth Front Army's fifty thousand fresh, well-rested troops to the Long March, but Chang had no liking for Mao's plan to continue journeying north to the Shensi Soviet. The only safe route of escape from pursuing Nationalist armies, he insisted, lay west toward Sikang or Tibet. To Mao this was "flightism" —a polite term for cowardice, but short of declaring civil war on Chang, Mao had no way to impose his will.

So the two leaders coolly agreed to go their separate ways with their respective armies. Surprisingly, Chu Teh now left Mao to join Chang. He later told journalist Agnes Smedley that Chang had forced him to join the Fourth Front Army at gunpoint. If there were other reasons, no one ever found out what they were, nor did Mao ever say.

Once more Mao set off with his forces, heading now for the Great Grasslands, a vast swamp occupied by autonomous tribes. The Queen of the Mant-ze tribe had issued orders that anyone who made contact with the Chinese, Red or White, would be boiled alive. Frightened tribesmen fled before the Red Army advance, leaving behind empty houses of dried mud. When Mao's men marched through narrow defiles, hidden tribesmen attacked them by rolling down huge boulders.

On the 329th day of the Long March a company of Reds was sent through the tall, fog-shrouded grasses, swinging swords. They were never seen again. Once a soldier called out to his comrades that he had found a sheep hiding in the grasses. When they slashed their way toward him, they were felled with poisoned arrows in their necks. In the eerie grasslands, it was clear, Mao's propaganda teams would win no hearts and minds.

Incessant rains made the desolate marshes even more sodden. There were no trees, no firewood. Horses stumbled and sank in the bottomless mud. The troops were often separated in heavy fog that blanketed the plains, and Mao often had to shout aloud to guide his column.

Some men fell into deep quicksand pits and disappeared without a trace. Those who tried to help were sucked into the treacherous bogs. At night many soldiers slept on their feet, tied together back to back like bundles of firewood, as distant wolves howled mournfully in the cold, rainy night.

Soon the rations of green wheat, raw beets, and turnips they had brought along from Mouking were gone. "We killed our livestock and our horses so that we might eat," Mao later told American author Robert Payne, "and we loaded their flesh on the few animals we had kept to carry the baggage. At the end, we had eaten even these and carried the flesh ourselves. Our most terrible enemies were the native tribes. It was from our contact with them that we learned the most. We have to thank the Generalissimo for having driven us into these foreign regions. Without him, we would never have seen them."

By the 341st day they were surviving on grass roots and soups made out of grass or boiled leather belts. Many died of starvation or poisoning. When one soldier found a hidden basketful of pigskins in an empty cottage, he began cutting them up as shoe soles for his comrades. Boiling them to loosen the bristles, he tasted the slices. Finding them edible, he prepared a meal of them instead. "One of our more successful banquets," Mao smiled.

Sloshing through the grasslands mud made their legs swell with red blisters. Huge mosquitoes tortured them day and night. All medical supplies had been used or lost. The ill who fell had to be left to die because none had the strength to carry them out of the vast black and yellow grass swamps. By the 352d day all regimental radios were out of order. Whole columns became lost.

Of the one hundred thousand Chinese who had started the Long March with Mao from Juichin only seven thousand emerged with him from the ordeal of the grasslands. Reaching Kansu, they were given shelter and rest in Tibetan mud houses, where they dried their soaked rags and caught up on sleep.

Here they were joined by some troops from Chang Kuo-t'ao's Fourth Front Army, which had been routed and put to flight by Nationalist troops supported by Moslem cavalry. These KMT forces were now the last barrier between Mao and the Red bases in Shensi Province.

He called upon his exhausted followers for one last act of courage and endurance. Crossing the Minshan Mountains, they ran into a blockade of enemy forces. Feinting a column to the west to lure them in that direction, Mao sought to break out toward the northeast. There he was attacked by the fierce cavalry of warlord Ma Hung-kuei.

As these Moslem Tartars of the Chinese Steppes started

their charge down a steep hill, concealed Red machine guns opened up on both their flanks. Frightened, their shaggy ponies bolted in all directions, throwing riders and rolling down the slopes with them. The Red Army counterattacked, and Ma Hung-kuei's demoralized forces fled. With them vanished Chiang Kai-shek's last hope of crushing Mao and his men.

At a small village in Shensi Province there was food for them—golden-colored millet. Some who had been dreaming of rice grumbled that they didn't know how to cook such stuff.

"Learn," said Mao. "If we don't adapt to new ways of living here in the north, we'll simply perish."

On October 20, 1935, Mao's columns, headed by hundreds of Red Army soldiers mounted on captured Moslem ponies, pulled up at the foot of the Great Wall in northern Shensi. Here they were met by five men on horseback carrying tommy-guns on their hips and wearing white towels on their heads.

"Welcome, Chairman Mao," said their leader. "We represent the Provincial Soviet of Northern Shensi. We have been waiting for you anxiously. All that we have, and our three Communist armies, are at your disposal."

The Long March was over at last, after six thousand miles. Mao's thoughts at that historic moment can only be conjectured. Was he thinking perhaps of his two children left behind with peasant guardians en route, like all the other children of the Long March? Of most of their mothers who had been left behind in graves, killed in battle, like Chu Teh's wife? One of the few female survivors who reached Shensi was Mao's wife, suffering severely from fourteen wounds.

Hospital wards at the village of Paoan quickly filled with Mao's sick and wounded. Because medicines were scarce in this remote region, Mao decided they would have to push

on still further as soon as possible. His hosts were puzzled.
"But where will you find medical supplies?"
"We will take them from the Japanese," Mao explained.

China was electrified by news that the Red Army had
broken through every blockade Chiang Kai-shek had
thrown in their path. In snatching a brilliant military victory
out of the jaws of defeat Mao and his men had made a
forced march through eleven provinces—Fukien, Kangsi,
Kwangtung, Hunan, Kwangsi, Kweichow, Yunnan, Sikang, Szechwan, Kansu, and Shensi.

"Wherever we went the peasants understood that we
were with them," Mao declared, "and if they ever doubted
it, the behavior of the Kuomintang soldiers soon persuaded
them." Throughout their passage the Red Army had stirred
the winds of change that would gradually build into a cy-
clone.

Mao celebrated the Long March with a proud poem:

The Red Army fears not the rigors of a forced march;
To them a thousand mountains, ten thousand rivers, are but a gentle
walk.
The Five Ridges ripple by like little waves,
And the mountain peaks of Wumeng are but mounds.
Warm are the cloud-topped cliffs above the River of Golden Sand,
Soft are the iron chains that span the Tatu River.
Soldiers delight in the ageless snows of Minshan,
And they smile proudly as the Army crosses.

During the winter of 1935–1936 at Paoan in the Shensi-
Kansu-Ninghsia Border Region, Mao lived in a cave, sleeping in a brick bed warmed with wood or hay beneath it.
Working thirteen or fourteen hours a day, he then read
books on philosophy and military strategy through most of
the night. With so much to do, so much still to learn, sleep
wasted valuable time.

In December, 1935, he called a CCP Politburo conference at Wayaopao in northern Shensi, at which he stressed the importance of pressing Chiang Kai-shek to call off the war on Chinese Communists and join with them in forging a United Front to smash the Japanese invasion. Skeptics asked for specific tactics. How could Mao expect Chiang, who had pursued the Long March vengefully for over a year, now suddenly to develop a halo and offer to embrace the Red Army instead?

The answer, Mao said, was to persuade the warlords under Chiang's command to put pressure on him by pointing out that the primary threat to their rule came from Tokyo, which was conquering China piecemeal, not from weak Red forces. Meanwhile the Red Army in the north must begin to fight against the Japanese on their own, proving to the Chinese people—and the warlords—that they were the real patriots.

"For a people being deprived of their national freedom, the revolutionary task is not immediate socialism, but the struggle for independence," Mao pointed out. "We cannot even discuss communism if we are robbed of a country in which to practice it."

In early 1936 he led his forces across the Yellow River to seize positions from which to launch an attack against the Japanese. They were driven back, however, when Chiang ordered an all-out offensive against them by his northern warlords. The Japanese, he told the warlords, were only "a sickness of the flesh," while the Communists were "a sickness of the heart." He condemned Mao's appeal for unity as a trick to win popular support and cautioned them "not to fall into the trap."

One of the most important of his generals, "Young Marshal" Chang Hsueh-liang, found himself under strong pressure from his troops, however, who opposed fighting any countrymen—Reds or otherwise—while the Japanese occupied Manchuria. In June, 1936, he was persuaded to meet with Chou En-lai, who convinced him to enter an anti-Japanese alliance with Mao.

Chang Hsueh-liang then sought to convince Chiang Kai-shek to follow this example. The Kuomintang leader angrily refused and warned the Young Marshal he was seriously jeopardizing the security of China by dealing with Mao.

On Mao's orders, meanwhile, Chou En-lai set up a "Northwest Anti-Japanese Red Army University" to train cadres for guerrilla warfare against the invaders. Lecturing them, Mao taught that space filled with mountains, swamp, or jungle was ideal terrain for guerrilla warfare against mechanized troops.

"China is a vast country," he explained. "When it is dark in the east, it is light in the west. When things are dark in the south, there is still light in the north. Hence one need not worry about lack of room to maneuver."

In December, 1936, an irate Chiang Kai-shek flew to Sian to discipline the Young Marshal and force him back into line. Asleep in a villa outside Sian, he was awakened by gunfire as the Young Marshal's troops forced their way past his guard to seize him and bring him to Sian as a prisoner.

"You must join us, General," Chang Hsueh-liang insisted firmly, "in the fight against the Japanese."

"If I am your general," Chiang Kai-shek snapped furiously, "then you must obey me! If you are my enemy, then kill me. Choose between those two alternatives!"

Mao rushed Chou En-lai to Sian to assure Chiang that he would be released unharmed if he promised to turn his armies against Japan. The alternative was not spelled out, but Chiang was no fool. He agreed sullenly. The Young Marshal then flew him to Nanking, where Chiang unenthusiastically announced an end to KMT attacks on the

Communists. But Mao had given him a concession to sweeten the pill. The Red Army would henceforth fight the Japanese in a United Front under the command of their erstwhile foe, Chiang Kai-shek.

Mao now felt free to move the Communists at Paoan into the little yellow-earth city of Yenan, a three-day hike along mountain trails. Here, two hundred miles from Sian, the nearest town, steep mountains and gorges protected him from a sudden change of mind by Chiang.

Yenan was to be Mao's headquarters for the next eleven years. Located on the banks of a gorge-enclosed river, it was a city of cave homes carved out of the surrounding cliffs by peasants in a region where building materials were scarce.

He set up his headquarters in a snug little whitewashed three-room cave, honeycombed in a sandstone hill that faced a date-tree orchard. Mao and his wife, Ho Tzu-chen, lived in the inner chamber, and Chou En-lai and another Chinese leader shared the outer chamber, made odoriferous by vats of pickles. The third room was a little office with a shaky table, battered wicker armchair, low sofa with bad springs, and a marked military wall map of China. These Spartan cave quarters remained Mao's home until sensational events in 1949.

Here he continued to live humbly and simply, eating the same meals as his troops—rice, wild vegetables, and soup —except that he also indulged his fondness for red pepper. Under a tattered blue cloak he wore a drab, baggy, much-patched uniform of cotton spun by local peasant women, with nothing to distinguish him as head of the Communist government and Red Army except his unusual height. He moved unostentatiously among Yenanites who accepted him casually as a comrade who happened to have the job of running things. The cult of Mao worship was a later development.

Children raced in and out of his cave at will, helping

themselves to homemade candy on his table. Anyone could speak to him, and he would offer a soft, smiling reply while absentmindedly chain-smoking harsh hand-rolled cigarettes.

In a small plot of ground near his cave he grew tobacco for himself and his friends. In the adjacent plot Chu Teh cultivated a cabbage patch. Mao persuaded all Red officials to do some physical labor regularly, emphasizing the bond of equality that should unite all Red intellectuals, workers, farmers, and soldiers.

Yenan became Mao's experimental laboratory for his ideas about a new life-style for the Chinese people, which he developed with the CCP Central Committee across a shabby red-felt tablecloth, their faces candle-illuminated. Opium was barred; cooperatives organized; child marriages forbidden; schooling made available to young and old alike.

Developing Yenan as the new Red capital, Mao created a university, a war academy, a publishing house, hospitals, and shops, all dug out of the rock like troglodytes' dwellings. Students came from all over China to attend the lectures on military strategy and literature that Mao gave personally. He urged patience on the most radical, advocating careful planning for the day when all China would be under the Red Star. He reminded enthusiastic Red Army volunteers that they must be the servants, not the masters, of the Chinese people. In the security and prestige that Mao now found at Yenan, however, he was blind to the great disadvantage of isolation which was to serve China poorly when he finally won his bid for power.

# Chapter 8

# "Washington Won, Didn't He?"

Mao spent much of his time reading, writing his thoughts on pieces of birch bark, and contemplating nature from his terrace. The view from his mountain cave was an austere little world that included his vegetable and tobacco patch, the date-tree orchard, the gully of Yenan, villagers working in their fields, the Yen River, and treeless brown mountains.

Gazing at this limited view for nearly eleven years, Mao's thoughts understandably dwelt on rural China, almost as though its cities and the world beyond did not exist. Until his visit to Chungking in 1945 he saw no city lights in all that time.

This severe isolation unquestionably influenced Mao's outlook, restricting his knowledge of and contacts with the West to books. Yenan walled him off not only from the capitalist nations, but also from the Soviet Union. Here were the roots of an intense Chinese provincialism that would later blind Mao to the changing nature of western society. He continued to judge it through the eyes of the nineteenth-century Marxists and sociologists that he read avidly in Yenan.

Theirs were the views he echoed when he described

China's plight in December, 1936: "China's political and economic development is uneven—a weak capitalist economy coexists with a preponderant semi-feudal economy; a few modern industrial and commercial cities coexist with a vast stagnant countryside; several million industrial workers coexist with several hundred millions of peasants and handicraftsmen. . . . A few railways, steamship lines and motor roads exist side by side with a vast number of wheelbarrow paths and footpaths."

He rejected, however, the Marxist view that Asia was so hopelessly backward and stagnant that it was incapable of modernizing except under the guidance of a western proletariat. "If we copy their rules and apply them mechanically, allowing no change whatsoever," Mao objected, "it will be like whittling down the feet to fit the shoes, and we shall be defeated." The Chinese, he asserted, must and could solve their own problems their own way. As proof he offered the military disasters that had befallen the Chinese Communists when the CCP Politburo insisted on obeying orders from Moscow. Mao admitted that he, too, had made mistakes but at least knew how to learn from them and change course.

The China he visualized would be an independent great power, not a Soviet satellite. "We are certainly not fighting for an emancipated China," he declared flatly, "in order to turn the country over to Moscow!"

In his lectures at Yenan's war academy he emphasized that no amount of book study could equal the practical experience of battlefield "exercises" against the Japanese. "To learn warfare through warfare—this is our chief method," he explained. He also warned against trusting hopeful slogans instead of hard facts: "A careless military man bases his plans on his own wishful thinking, and hence his plans are fanciful and do not correspond to reality."

Mao's students, flocking to Yenan from all over China, were eager to become part of a new Spartan army in which officers were merely "leaders" with no distinguishing rank and ate the same food as enlisted men. Any private could see Chu Teh, who earned ninety cents a month as Commanding General, to voice a grievance or request. Punishment for military offenses consisted of only confinement to quarters, public rebuke and self-criticism, or expulsion from the Red Army. Soldiers fought in the Red Army not for their twenty-cent monthly pay, but because they sincerely believed that they were defending their country against the Japanese and/or for socialist ideals. Their high morale was the essential difference between them and the forces of either Chiang or Tokyo.

In his strategy against the Japanese Mao used the same elusive tactics that had proved so successful against Chiang during the Long March. In vain did the enemy seek to find and engage the Red Army in full-scale battle. Whenever the Japanese took a town, moreover, Mao organized the countryside around them to try to starve them out.

The invaders were most dumbfounded by the Red Army's amazing ability to arm themselves with enemy weapons. "We rely on the war industries of the imperialist countries and of our enemy at home," Mao told his troops in December, 1936. "We have a claim on the output of the arsenals of London as well as of Hanyang, and what is more, it is to be delivered to us by the enemy's own transport corps. This is the sober truth, not a joke."

Mao's greatest weapon of all, however, was the faith of the Chinese peasantry in his incorruptibility. The courteous, helpful behavior of the Red Army in the countryside counted heavily in Mao's favor. So did his setting up, in guerrilla-controlled areas, local governments made up of one-third Communists, one-third other political leaders, and one-third nonparty peasants. In many ways these communities operated more democratically than those elsewhere in China.

Japanese atrocities drove more and more Chinese into supporting the Red Army. In July, 1937, Tokyo intensified its invasion. Chinese suspected of resisting were kicked, beaten, forced to dig their own graves, and then either buried alive or decapitated. Many were killed simply for failing to bow before parading Japanese troops swiftly or deeply enough.

The rage of the Chinese people was now so great that Chiang knew he would be overthrown if he dared go back on his word to join the Red Army in fighting the Japanese. On September 27, 1937, he signed an agreement establishing the United Front. Under it Chiang also agreed to end all attacks on the Red Army, release all political prisoners, and improve living conditions and democratic liberties in regions under his control. In return Mao promised to stop seeking to overthrow the KMT government, end his campaign against landlordism, and put the Fourth and Eighth Red armies under Chiang's command as a new Eighth Route Army in blue Nationalist uniforms.

Now opposition to Mao's policies surfaced once again in the CCP Central Committee. Hard-line leftists criticized him for collaboration with the Nationalist "monster" who had mercilessly massacred Communists at Shanghai and who had sought to wipe out the rest during the Long March.

Mao rejected their complaints as shortsighted, pointing out that all China now admired the Communists for subordinating ideology to patriotism. The United Front might postpone the struggle for socialism temporarily but only to save China for an inevitable Red future.

The new Eighth Route Army went into action against the Japanese even before the ink on the treaty with Chiang dried. Split into one-thousand- and two-thousand-man units behind Japanese lines, they began waging a skillful campaign of guerrilla warfare. Evidence of the enthusiasm they aroused among the Chinese people was unmistakable in their growth from a force of fifty thousand to five hundred thousand in the next eight years.

Tokyo's powerful armies, nevertheless, overran all the great coastal cities of China by the summer of 1938. Chiang fell back prudently, holding his Nationalist forces in reserve and leaving most of the fighting to the Eighth Route Army. The leopard had changed his tactics, not his spots.

At Communist headquarters in Yenan, meanwhile, Mao found himself absorbed in more than just the war. Her name was Chiang Ch'ing, although it was Blue Apple when she had been a divorced movie actress in Shanghai. Invited to Yenan to direct the Red Army theater, she had immediately attracted Mao's eye. Their meeting, according to one Chinese report, had been like "dried firewood on roaring fire." Charmed by the cool confidence of the twenty-four-year-old actress, who dressed plainly in a pajamalike outfit belted at her slim waist, the infatuated Mao determined to dissolve his marriage to Ho Tzu-chen and marry the glamorous newcomer.

Politburo leaders were outraged. They respected Mao's wife as a loyal and courageous comrade of the heroic Long March days and suspected Chiang Ch'ing of political ambitions. They refused to approve until she promised that she would keep out of party affairs and the public eye.

Ho Tzu-chen then dutifully left Yenan for Moscow, ostensibly to get medical treatment for her old war wounds. She divorced Mao there, freeing him to marry. Chiang Ch'ing bore Mao two children and kept her promise to stay aloof from public affairs for the next twenty-six years.

At the same time as he took a new wife, Mao bade farewell to his sole surviving brother. Mao Tse-min left Yenan to become treasurer for a local warlord who was then collaborating with the Soviet Union. When the warlord later changed his allegiance, Tse-min was arrested and executed.

From 1938 to 1940 Mao left the military campaign against Japan largely in the capable hands of Chu Teh and devoted most of his time to deep reflection as he sought to blueprint the future course of Marxism in China. Morning bugles that woke most of Yenan often found him busy writing by candlelight as dawn in the desert-blue sky illuminated the yellow-earth caves.

Now those around him were no longer free to disturb his meditations. A matter had to be weighty before the phone in his cave office was allowed to ring. Although he was still as gentle-mannered as ever, he spent hours lost in his own thoughts, stroking his chin reflectively.

In 1938 he wrote a small manual for the Red Army called *Basic Tactics,* explaining how to fight a guerrilla war against a formal army like that of the Japanese. "Avoid strength," he taught, "and strike at weakness." It was also more important for guerrilla forces to kill troops than to take territory.

"When we see the enemy, we must not be frightened to death like a rat who sees a cat," Mao wrote, "simply because he has a weapon in his hands. . . . We are men, the enemy is also composed of men, we are all men, so what should we fear? The fact that he has weapons? We can find a way to seize his weapons. All we are afraid of is getting killed by the enemy. But when we undergo the oppression of the enemy . . . how can anyone still fear death? And if we do not fear death, then what is there to fear about the enemy?"

At the same time he cautioned the Red Army to melt away in the face of powerful Japanese offensives. In a tract called *On Protracted War* (May, 1938) he wrote, "Undoubtedly, if we are to avoid decisive engagements, we shall have to abandon territory. . . . Trading space for time is correct. History tells us how Russia made a courageous retreat to avoid a decisive engagement and then defeated Napoleon, the terror of his age. Today China should do likewise."

He added, "Not that we would not like a quick victory; everybody would be in favor of driving the 'devils' out overnight. But . . . the only way to final victory is the strategy of protracted war."

Chiang Kai-shek did not need *On Protracted War* to encourage his hasty retreat before advancing Japanese forces. In 1938 he abandoned Nanking to them and fled inland to Chungking. To slow their advance he blew up dikes drowning eleven cities and four thousand villages, bringing death and misery to some twelve million peasants. Chiang's brand of "national defense" did not endear him the more to the Chinese people.

With the coastal cities of China in their hands the Japanese stripped them of booty. Convoys sailed for Tokyo loaded with pianos, furniture, refrigerators, art treasures, food, and machinery. Chinese men, women, and children were used as slave labor by sword-slashing taskmasters.

Behind the Japanese lines now only the Eighth Route Army remained an effective Chinese military and political force. Guerrilla leaders followed Mao's manual in keeping the enemy off balance: "Ingenious devices such as making a noise in the east while attacking in the west, appearing now in the south and now in the north, hit-and-run and night action should be constantly employed to mislead, entice and confuse the enemy."

In contrast to Nationalist forces the Red guerrillas never pillaged villages or stripped peasants of good boots. Living only on grains and vegetables they paid for, they left peasant wells, livestock, and harvests untouched. Peasant youth flocked to join them, and a whole new Fourth Route Army was assembled behind enemy lines.

"Many people think it is impossible for guerrillas to exist long in the enemy's rear," Mao observed. "Such a belief reveals a lack of comprehension of the relationship that should exist between the people and troops. The former may be likened to water and the latter to fish who swim in it."

In Hopei early in 1939 a well-developed Communist government functioned as a new Red "island" inside Japanese-occupied territory. The people fed, sheltered, and doctored the guerrillas; cooperated in sabotage; and served as spies and scouts for Mao's forces. They drove the Japanese wild by removing and burying train rails.

"With the common people of the whole country mobilized," Mao wrote confidently, "we shall create a vast sea of humanity and drown the enemy in it."

Some foreign observers with the Japanese scoffed at the idea of Mao's "ragamuffin army" defeating Tokyo's powerful forces in China. Mao replied, "It's true the enemy has electricity, airplanes and tanks, and we have nothing. But then, the British had everything and George Washington had nothing. Yet Washington won, didn't he? So shall we!"

Chiang Kai-shek viewed the spread of Communist-occupied territory behind Japanese lines with increasing misgivings, despite Mao's claim to be controlling it in the name of the Nationalist government. Chiang was also worried by the growing popularity and stature of Mao as a national hero.

He gave secret orders to his warlords to suppress all Communist organizations in Kuomintang territory, and to seal off Mao's headquarters in Yenan from the rest of China, he organized an undeclared military and economic blockade around the Border Region. The CCP angrily accused Chiang of sabotaging the United Front agreement. He could not be held accountable, he replied frostily, for the "individual" actions of warlords he could not control from Chungking.

Mao now grimly ordered his Red Army commanders to

"gain control of as many districts as you can . . . from Nanking in the west to the sea coast in the east." Warning the Communists of Yenan that they were under siege, he urged every woman, child, soldier, student, and official to join Yenan's peasants and shopworkers in making their province self-sufficient as quickly as possible.

Everyone worked long, hard hours, eating little and wearing old clothes until they literally fell apart. New Uniforms for soldiers were made on sewing machines captured from the Japanese. There was little or no aid from the Soviet Union, which was hoarding its own resources against a feared attack by Nazi Germany.

Mao was startled when Stalin suddenly signed a nonaggression pact with Hitler in August, 1939, but he accepted the Soviet explanation that this treaty had foiled a western plot to goad Nazi Germany into attacking Moscow. Mao hoped that Stalin would now feel free to come to his aid, but he soon realized that Stalin was interested in acting only in Russia's behalf, viewing other revolutionary struggles through that prism alone. Mao's conviction deepened that China must find its own way toward socialism.

In 1940 he wrote *On the New Democracy,* proclaiming the uniqueness of the Chinese revolutionary movement. The Yenan experiment, he declared, proved that the Chinese version of Marxism was best for backward agrarian countries. He also challenged the Soviet concept of revolutionary stages: that feudalism must first be overthrown by capitalism, then capitalism by socialism. Not so, Mao wrote. In China both revolutions were going on simultaneously.

The audacity of *On the New Democracy* staggered the Kremlin. Was this little Chinese upstart locked into Yenan by Chiang's warlords presuming to challenge the mighty Joseph Stalin for leadership of the Communist world? The *Times of London* managed to get an interview with Mao. Its correspondent asked him to describe his vision of socialism in China.

"Every man has food to eat and clothes to wear," Mao replied. "Every man understands the rights and duties of citizenship and has a fair chance of education and amusement. The marriage customs are to be reformed, roads built, industry developed, a six-hour day established. There is no foreign aggression. No man oppresses another. There is equality and freedom and universal love. Together all build the peace of the world." He added, "No one'll get anywhere here if he's after promotion, or out to make a fortune."

A new problem for Mao arose when the Japanese in Nanking set up a puppet Chinese government, which then announced that China would soon sign a negotiated peace with Japan. It was now obviously urgent to prove to the Chinese people that the struggle against Japan must, and would, go on.

In August, 1940, Mao launched one hundred simultaneous attacks by four hundred thousand Eighth and Fourth Route army troops against Japanese forces in North China. These troop movements brought the Communists into collision with many Nationalist divisions still blockading Yenan on Chiang's secret orders.

Surrounding nine thousand men of the Fourth Route Army in January, 1941, Nationalists wiped them out in a ten-day battle. Chiang Kai-shek then ordered the rest of the Fourth Route Army to disband. Mao defied the directive, bitterly accusing Chiang of having martyred Communist troops whose only crime had been trying to drive out the invaders of their country. The United Front was dead.

The Japanese, infuriated by Mao's "100 Regiments Offensive," mounted a powerful campaign against the Communist-controlled countryside of North China in July,

1941. Operating under a "three-all" policy—"burn all, kill all, loot all"—the Japanese not only wiped out a fourth of the Eighth Route Army but also destroyed tens of thousands of villages and killed 20 million civilians out of a 45 million population. *That* would teach the Communists a lesson!

There was no word of protest from Chiang Kai-shek.

# The Americans Visit Mao

Tokyo's overconfident militarists now decided to join their fortunes to those of Adolf Hitler, who had torn up his pact with Stalin and sent his divisions crashing into the Soviet Union. Nazi Germany was clearly fated to rule the western hemisphere; Japan would rule Asia as a partner. Together they would crush the last obstacle, the United States.

On December 7, 1941, the Japanese struck at Pearl Harbor. The whole world picture suddenly changed as the American people found themselves plunged into World War II as allies of the Chinese, Russians, British, and Free French.

Eager for American aid, Stalin sought to sooth Washington's fears of his plans for world revolution. On March 5, 1942, he sent a cable to Mao insisting that he must patch up his differences with the Nationalists, regardless of Chiang's unreliability. Mao was enough of a realist to know that Pearl Harbor had changed everything. With American aid the Japanese could now be driven out of China in a few years, instead of several decades. On his persuasion the CCP Central Committee now worked out a truce with the KMT government.

At the same time, Mao sought to strengthen North China as a revolutionary bastion. He insisted that its intellectuals come down out of their cultural ivory towers and live with the common people, devoting their creative efforts to advancing the class struggle against all enemies.

In a Yenan Forum speech on Chinese art and literature in May, 1942, he told them, "You must go to the people, must strive to understand them before you can ever hope to have them understand you. You must learn to love them for what they are, not for what you think they should be."

Art and literature, he insisted, must become revolutionary weapons "to help the people fight the enemy with one heart and one mind." Not that art-for-art's-sake classics of the past were to be despised. But a new time called for a new type of classics, reflecting the aspirations of the masses.

"Will not Marxism-Leninism then destroy the creative spirit?" he asked. "Oh, yes, it will. It will destroy . . . the creative spirit that is rooted in liberalism, individualism . . . art for art's sake. . . . Any brand of creative spirit which is not of the masses and of the proletariat . . . should be destroyed . . . to make room for the new."

Mao also appealed to women, youth, and the peasantry to enlist in the class struggle. "You must realize," he told André Malraux later, "that before us, among the masses, no one had addressed themselves to women or to the young. Nor, of course, to the peasants. For the first time in their lives, every one of them felt *involved.*"

Despite his truce with Chiang, Mao launched an "expositions of bitterness" campaign to extend Communist influence in areas abandoned to the Japanese by fleeing Nationalist troops. Communist cadres, moving in behind Japanese lines, would hold secret village meetings at which peasants related their sufferings under Nationalist warlords, whipping up hatred against their former oppressors.

"We organized these expositions in every village," Mao acknowledged. Peasants were persuaded to support Red Army guerrillas against both Japanese and Nationalists because "communism is first of all an insurance against fascism."

Mao's prestige soared steadily as Chiang's went into decline. From Chungking United States Ambassador Clarence Gauss gave his estimate of the situation to Washington:

> At present, the generalissimo is losing the support of China. His orders are not carried out. He has difficulty collecting enough food for his immense army and bureaucracy. From top to bottom, the structure of his government is riddled with open corruption. . . . He knows that he cannot conquer the Communists without foreign aid.
>
> Thus he will do everything he can to force us to give him active assistance, which would risk involving us not only in a civil war in China, but also in a conflict with Russia. . . . The Communists will be the dominant power in China in a few years. . . . The destiny of China is in their hands, not in those of Chiang Kai-shek.

For 1942 that was a remarkably prescient prediction.

Stalin, meanwhile, continued to do everything possible to reassure his capitalist allies that it was safe to help him fight off Hitler; that he was not dedicated to overthrowing their governments. Hoping to encourage them to open a second front in 1943 by invading occupied France, he announced the dissolution of the Communist International (Comintern).

To Mao that was also good news because, formally at least, Moscow had renounced the right to give orders to the Chinese Communists. Stalin's concession had weakened the hands of Mao's Stalinist rivals in the CCP Central Committee. Mao hailed Stalin's decision as a wise one, even though, he added with a straight face, the Comintern had never "meddled" in the internal affairs of the CCP. It was a subtle way of putting Stalin on notice that any future attempt to dictate policy to the CCP would be considered meddling by Mao.

Once self-effacing and almost saintly in his modesty, Mao began to undergo subtle changes in his character during the war years. His triumphs of survival over the powerful opposition of his enemies Chiang and the Japanese, and his rivals Stalin and the CCP Stalinists, had been little less than miraculous. He began to feel omnipotent.

*Nothing* could destroy him, he now felt confident, simply because his long years of study and reflection had made him far wiser than those who sought to bring him down. It only remained to convince the Chinese people to unite solidly behind him, and his superior strategy and tactics would lead them to freedom and make China once more a great nation.

A new element also entered his strategy with the emergence of America as a war ally. Washington had named Chiang Kai-shek supreme commander of the Chinese theater, including Thailand and Indo-China. But, Mao mused, the United States was bound to become disillusioned with Chiang once Washington realized that he was nothing but a corrupt dictator with no taste for fighting the Japanese. Why not a shift of policy that could give the Americans a reasonable alternative?

They, after all, had fought a revolutionary struggle to free their own country and then had built a democratic system of government. Mao saw no reason why, by simply changing his emphasis, he could not follow that example. Socialism could be introduced into China just as well through democracy as through a revolutionary dictatorship. If the Americans could be made to sympathize with Mao's revolutionary struggle, especially since it entailed vigorously fighting and defeating Japan, Mao might emerge from the war as Washington's choice to lead a new China.

United States Lieutenant General Joseph W. Stilwell was appointed Chiang Kai-shek's chief of staff and was also put in charge of operations against the Japanese in the north of Burma. He was a blunt, intelligent soldier who had spent thirteen years in China, spoke the Mandarin dialect, and understood the Chinese people.

Flying back and forth between New Delhi and Chungking, he was constantly frustrated in his efforts to compel Chiang to fight the Japanese. Equally futile were his attempts to force Chiang to purge his corrupt generals. Despairing of the Nationalists, Stilwell finally demanded to be allowed to visit Yenan to arrange cooperation with Mao's Eighth Route Army. Impossible, murmured Chiang.

The Nationalist leader issued secret orders to all his generals to ignore Stilwell's commands. When the American general came roaring in anger to Chungking, Chiang pretended to be puzzled by his warlords' "foolish" failure to obey.

Their loyalty to Chiang was assured by the wealthy rackets he let them operate. They sold United States military aid, including food, on the black market; robbed their own troop payrolls; smuggled opium, gas, and cloth; sold draft exemptions to well-to-do families; and used the Chinese Red Cross to obtain and sell medical supplies.

Nationalist troop morale, understandably, was low. Ordered to attack Communist units instead of the Japanese, whole companies of KMT soldiers deserted to the Eighth Route Army. Mao's forces once wryly returned over one hundred rifles to Chiang with a note adhering to the United Front: "We can't force your men to return, but here are their arms."

Chiang preserved face by permitting no one to ask questions or discuss his decrees. Madame Chiang was even more imperious in her many roles as his adviser, translator, diplomat, and even commander of his air forces. "Not only God," she once wrote cynically, "but everybody else is on the side of the big battalions." She offered to have Stilwell promoted to four-star general if he agreed to support her demand for increased American aid to the Kuomintang.

Frustrated at every turn, Stilwell denounced "Peanuts" and "Madame the Empress"—his nicknames for the Chiangs—for the total corruption of their regime. He raged to United States Army Chief of Staff General George Marshall that Chiang was an "obstinate, pig-headed, ignorant, arbitrary, unreasonable, illogical . . . head of a one-party government supported by a Gestapo and a party secret service."

"Through a series of clever maneuvers," Stilwell wrote bitterly, "we have been put in the position of supporting this rotting regime and glorifying its representative, the omniscient, the great patriot and soldier: Peanuts! What we should do is shoot the generalissimo."

When Chiang attended the Cairo Conference in November, 1943, his arrogant demands exasperated General Marshall. "Now let me get this straight," the Army Chief of Staff exploded. "You are talking about your 'rights.' . . . I thought these were *American* planes and *American* personnel, and *American* matériel. I don't understand what you mean that *we* can or can't do thus and so!"

Stilwell reported that Chiang "hates the so-called Communists. He intends to crush them by keeping any munitions furnished him. . . . He will not make an effort to fight seriously. He wants to finish the war coasting, with a big supply of material, so as to perpetuate his regime."

Chiang hated Stilwell for exposing his scheme but felt no need to make even a pretense of fighting the Japanese. The United States would be forced to do the job itself anyway, so why not save his strength to finish off the Communists?

"Chiang Kai-shek is . . . bewildered by the spread of Communist influence," Stilwell told Marshall. "He can't see that the mass of Chinese people welcome the Reds as being the only visible hope of relief from crushing taxation, the abuses of the army. . . . Under Chiang Kai-shek they now begin to see what they may expect. Greed, corruption, favoritism, more taxes, a ruined currency, terrible waste of life, callous disregard of all the rights of men. . . . The cure for China's trouble is the elimination of Chiang Kai-shek. The only thing that keeps the country split is his fear of losing control."

As relations between Chiang and Washington worsened, Mao became more and more pro-American. On the Fourth of July, 1944, the Communist *Liberation Daily* praised the American democratic tradition. "The work which we Communists are carrying on today," said its editorial, "is the very same work which was carried on earlier in America by Washington, Jefferson and Lincoln." Mao was now hopeful that United States disillusionment with Chiang would result in the rechanneling of at least some aid for China to Yenan instead of Chungking.

Although both Marshall and President Roosevelt now knew the acid truth about Chiang, Stilwell's revelations were withheld from the American people. Chiang was still America's official ally, and it was feared that exposing him might result in a congressional uproar and public disillusionment. Billions in American aid had been given the Chinese leader certified by the administration as a fine "champion of Asian democracy" fighting gallantly against the Japanese.

In July, 1944, the President sent a liaison mission to Yenan to talk to Mao. From a small airstrip its members were transported to Mao's caves in a half-ton Chevrolet delivery truck donated by New York Chinese laundrymen and used as an ambulance. Mao met his visitors at the entrance of the small compound in which he lived with his family and aides.

The Americans found their host a tall, broad-shouldered Chinese with long blue-black hair, fine cheekbones, and a sweeping forehead. Looking more like forty than his fifty-one years, Mao smiled easily and talked with almost boyish enthusiasm.

He entertained his guests at a regular Saturday night dance held in an apple orchard at Communist party headquarters. Colored lanterns hung from spreading branches, and the dance floor was smoothed earth. The emancipation of women in Yenan was manifest when they selected dance partners, instead of waiting to be asked. The orchestra of fiddle, mouth organ, banjo, zither, musical saw, and pedal organ played Viennese waltzes, French minuets, and American fox-trots.

A shirt-sleeved Mao enjoyed himself dancing a fast waltz with his pretty wife Chiang Ch'ing while other veteran revolutionaries like Chu Teh and Chou En-lai pranced an even livelier pace. The Americans were fascinated by this glimpse of the lighthearted side of Red leaders who even then controlled the destinies of some ninety million Chinese.

The visitors were surprised to find pro-American, rather than pro-Soviet, feeling among the Yenan Communists. They also saw no Russian aid of any kind—no guns, planes, equipment, or advisers. Mao, they observed, did not act like a dictator, nor was he treated as one. The CCP Politburo, far from being a rubber stamp for Mao's views, often questioned them sharply and amended them. Mao emphasized that the Chinese Communists operated in a democratic fashion and smilingly called himself the Abraham Lincoln of China.

"We do not pretend that we are perfect," he told State Department official John S. Service. "We still face problems of bureaucracy and corruption. But we do face them. And we are beating them. We welcome observation and criticism—by the Americans, by the KMT or by anyone else. We are constantly criticizing ourselves and revising our policies."

Colonel David Barrett questioned the wisdom of giving political training to peasants who made up the Eighth Route Army. He pointed out that the American army believed in avoiding controversial politics as divisive, giving American G.I.'s military training only. Chu Teh politely begged to disagree. The soldier behind the gun must be motivated by political ideals. It was political training that made the difference between the highly dedicated Red Army guerrillas and the nonpolitical, unmotivated Nationalist troops.

Mao, however, assured the liaison mission that "we are no longer Communists in the Soviet Russian sense of the word." As proof he pointed to their democratic life-style and their tolerance (for the time being, at least) of landlords, merchants, capitalists, and petite bourgeoisie in areas they controlled. He would even welcome foreign capital and investments in Chinese trade and industry, he now declared, in order to help develop the country's backward economy rapidly.

The Americans were greatly impressed with Mao. They approved of his realistic goals for every Chinese village: a one-year grain reserve against drought, one spinning and weaving machine, one village blacksmith, one day and one night school, total literacy, a medical cooperative in every district, an ox and a pig for every family, a latrine in every household, at least one well in every village.

These goals were high dreams in a land where a brown steamed bun, issued twice a month, was considered a great luxury. Mao and his comrades regularly visited nearby villages to discuss these needs of peasants in their own earthy language, as well as to lend a hand with farm chores. "Our starting point," Mao declared in a speech in early 1945, "is to serve the Chinese people earnestly and wholeheartedly, and never to be severed from the people . . . not serving the interests of a small group or oneself."

If Mao was now winning American sympathy in some

high places, the United States lobby for Chiang was still powerful and had the status quo on their side. Roosevelt's advisers warned that it would be impossible to withdraw recognition from the Nationalists as the true government of China without causing chaos and crippling the war effort against Japan.

Meanwhile Chiang was issuing almost hysterical demands for the recall of his severest critic, General "Vinegar Joe" Stilwell. On the advice of a trusted adviser, General Patrick Hurley, the President yielded. Stilwell was recalled to Washington and warned to say nothing to the press.

Disappointed in Roosevelt's continued support of Chiang, Mao nevertheless sent a cable of sympathy when the President died. In his report to the CCP Seventh Congress ten days later, he praised the American war effort against Japan.

Mao's flirtation with the Americans as a Chinese "democrat" did not sit at all well with Stalin, especially when Mao publicly rejected the Soviet experience as a revolutionary model for China, endorsing democracy instead.

In April, 1945, Mao wrote *On Coalition Government,* calling now for the establishment of a bourgeois coalition democracy to govern postwar China. Not a one-party dictatorship, he insisted, but only an alliance of "several democratic classes" could put China on the road to eventual socialism. He called his program "New Democracy . . . a system which is distinguished from the Russian system, and which is perfectly necessary and reasonable for us."

Stalin's outraged roar was promptly heard in Yenan. CCP Stalinists accused Mao of having sold out to capitalism. He replied, "To replace the oppression of foreign imperialism and native feudalism with capitalism developed to a certain degree, is not only an advance but also an unavoidable process."

Hoping for the ear of the new American President,

Harry S Truman, Mao demanded an end to Chiang's one-party dictatorship and a guarantee of freedom of speech, press, assembly, association, and political and religious convictions. "In China," he declared, "it is only in the liberated areas that these freedoms are fully enjoyed."

If Mao sounded like the ideal Asian democrat, there were nevertheless signs at the Seventh CCP Congress that a Maoist personality cult was in the making. It was signaled by a major speech by Liu Shao-ch'i, the political commissar of the New Fourth Army, who praised Mao as "not only the greatest revolutionary and statesman in Chinese history, but also its greatest theoretician and scientist." As though that were not enough, Liu proposed Mao as the new spiritual leader of Asia: "The thought of Mao Tse-tung will make great and useful contributions to the struggle for the emancipation of the people of all countries . . . of the East in particular."

The Congress then adopted a new constitution, whose preamble sanctified "the Thought of Mao Tse-tung" as essential "to guide the entire work" of the Chinese Communist party. Such glorification was not displeasing to Mao's vanity. Indeed, there is reason to suspect that he inspired it. But more than mere vanity was involved. Mao knew that because of his New Democracy program, he faced a tug-of-war with the angry Stalinists in the CCP Politburo. They would find it much harder to defeat Mao, the sacrosanct idol worshiped by the Chinese people, than Mao the politician.

Significantly, he wrote an anonymous article in the Yenan press asserting that the people wanted to follow only "Mao Tse-tung's way." If only Truman would now dump Chiang and support Mao's proposal for a New Democracy, he reflected hopefully, a bright new day for China would dawn at last.

In June, 1945, he was shocked out of this dream by the sudden arrest of John S. Service, the State Department official who had spent six months in Yenan as part of the United States liaison mission to Mao. Service, dismayed by the official seal of silence about Chiang, had leaked the "top secret" mission report submitted to the State Department on the Chinese situation to an American magazine for publication.

Mao interpreted Service's arrest as a sign that Washington was determined to continue supporting Chiang at all costs. Why else was the United States government so intent upon suppressing information favorable to Mao? The Yenan press angrily warned that if the Truman administration tried to clamp the reactionary Kuomintang regime on the Chinese people, the Americans might have to be taught a lesson. "Since I have been able to fight Japan with a few rusty rifles," Mao told two American visitors coolly, "I can fight the Americans too if I have to."

He guessed that events would begin to move swiftly on August 6, 1945, when the United States dropped the world's first atom bomb on Hiroshima. Two days later Stalin rushed to win a seat at the Asian victory council by declaring war on Japan and speeding troops into Manchuria.

To Mao's disgust, Stalin signed a new Sino-Soviet Treaty not with the Chinese Communists, but with Chiang's Nationalists. More than the Kremlin leader's pique at Mao was involved. Stalin was convinced that with American support Chiang would emerge the ruler of postwar China.

Eight days after Hiroshima the war was over. China was free at last. The defeated Japanese prepared to turn back their conquered territory to the Chinese.

But to *which* Chinese?

# Chapter 10 口

# Revolution!

Preparing for his power struggle with Chiang, Mao sought to reassure the Communists of China that they could win any civil war Chiang forced on them, even if the Nationalists were backed by American atom bombs. He refused to credit the holocaust at Hiroshima for Japan's abrupt surrender.

"Can atom bombs decide wars?" he demanded. "No, they can't. Without the struggles waged by the people, atom bombs by themselves would be of no avail. . . . Why didn't Japan surrender when the two bombs were dropped on her, and why did she only when the Soviet Union sent troops? Some of our comrades, too, believe that the atom bomb is all-powerful; that is a big mistake."

Part of Mao's bravado was an attempt to calm hysterical fears of America's terrible new weapons and to reassure his people that they were not powerless against such might even if it should be turned against them. But he was also sincerely convinced that no mere military weapon, however destructive, could prevail over the determination of a people to be free.

He pointed out, moreover, that nuclear bombs were useless against agrarian countries. There were simply no big concentrated targets worth their immense cost, and so they could hardly be used to prevent Asian revolutions.

With the announcement of Japan's surrender Mao threw down the gauntlet to Chiang in a direct challenge. "To whom should the fruits of victory in the war of resistance belong?" he demanded. "It is very obvious. Take a peach tree, for example. . . . Who is entitled to pick the peaches? Ask, who planted and watered the tree? Chiang Kai-shek, squatting on the mountain, did not carry a single bucket of water, yet now he stretches out his arms from afar to pick the peaches. He says, 'I own them as the landlord. You are my serfs, and I won't allow you to pick any.' We say, 'You never carried any water, so you have no right to pick them!' "

Now Mao and Chiang began a race through North China to take over territory and arms being surrendered by the Japanese. Chiang angrily commanded all Red troops to remain where they were. But Chu Teh spearheaded columns toward Manchuria. Mao denounced Chiang as a "fascist ringleader, autocrat and traitor" who had cooperated with the enemy, instead of with his own countrymen against them.

The 20,000 survivors of the Long March had now grown to a postwar army of 910,000, who controlled nineteen "liberated areas" containing 90 million Chinese. The CCP itself now had 1.2 million active party members.

In the race for Japanese-abandoned territory Mao's forces had a great advantage. The Eighth Route Army, welcomed, fed, sheltered, and supplied by the people everywhere, was able to operate in small scattered units without the huge Quartermaster Corps that KMT troops required. Their greater mobility allowed them to beat the Nationalists to many territorial prizes, mustering local people to the Red banner.

Alarmed at the explosive situation, President Truman dispatched General Pat Hurley to China to persuade Chiang and Mao to bury their quarrel and agree on a coalition government. Flying to Yenan first in August, 1945, Hurley was greatly impressed by his meeting with Mao. "The Chinese Communists are not Communists at all," he reassured the President. "They are only New Dealers!"

Hurley told Mao that Chiang, under strong pressure from Washington, had agreed to negotiations with the Communists. He urged Mao to fly with him to Chungking, pledging that the American government would guarantee the safety of Mao and any delegation he led. Pressure from Moscow came in the form of a cable from Stalin acidly advising Mao to dissolve the Red Army and join the Kuomintang, because "the development of an uprising in China has no prospect of success." Translation from the Russian meant to Mao: "We won't help you."

Hoping to compel Chiang to recognize the CCP and its control of the liberated areas, Mao agreed to go to Chungking. "Chiang imagines that there can't be two suns in the sky, nor two sovereigns for a people," he told the Politburo, "but I'm determined to give him two suns to look at."

He was delighted by his first flight in a plane. He looked down on the snowcapped mountains he had crossed on foot eleven years earlier and wrote a poem:

> All the views in the north
> Are enclosed in masses of ice and whirling snow. . . .
> The mountains are dancing silver serpents,
> The hills on the plains are shining elephants. . . .
> The earth is so lovely,
> Like a red-cheeked girl arrayed in white.

When a correspondent later sought to discuss this and other of Mao's poems, Mao merely shrugged and smiled. "They're really terribly bad. I just write poetry to waste time."

As the plane lost altitude for the approach to Chungking, Mao stared at the scenes rushing by: peasants carting buckets of sweet potatoes, loads of wood, and bales of straw through fields to straw-roofed houses; water buffalo plowing flooded rice paddies in the ravines. "There," he said to Hurley, "is the *real* China—not the China of Chiang's palaces, warlords, and banks."

Soon after their arrival in Chungking, the Japanese surrender ceremony took place in Tokyo Bay aboard the United States battleship *Missouri.* China was represented only by a Nationalist general on Chiang's staff. Mao mildly pointed out to the embarrassed Hurley the fine irony of excluding representation for the only Chinese who had fought against the Japanese.

When the two Chinese enemy leaders finally met face to face for the first time in nineteen years, both behaved with impeccable tact. At diplomatic dinners they smiled at and toasted each other, just as though Mao had not labeled Chiang a traitor and fascist, and Chiang had not put a price of $250,000 on Mao's head as a Red criminal. The two men made a striking contrast: the well-groomed Chiang in his flawless, bemedaled uniform; the bearlike, awkward Mao in pith helmet and crumpled, baggy, severely plain Red Army uniform with no insignia.

Forty-three days of negotiations were lubricated by frequent banquets. Mao, who had seen no city lights in twenty years, would have been less than human if he had not enjoyed his business holiday. He was delighted when a Chungking youth delegation called to pay their respects. "Chairman Mao," said the blushing girl leader, "to express to you the highest respect of Chinese youth, please allow me to kiss your hand."

Some in Chungking were less ardent admirers, though. One night when Mao attended a classical opera, someone fired at his car parked outside the theater. His chauffeur was killed, the killer obviously under the impression that it was Mao at the wheel.

Mao worked long and patiently at reaching an understanding with Chiang. The Nationalist leader balked at Hurley's plan for a coalition government. Mao offered to drop his demand for participation if Chiang would agree to democratize his regime, ending his dictatorship. Chiang refused.

Mao then offered to yield up certain liberated areas and reduce his armed forces to twenty divisions if Chiang agreed to reduce the Nationalist Army proportionately. Chiang refused.

After six weeks of futile negotiations Chiang furiously accused Mao of wanting civil war. Hurley, chagrined by the failure of his mission, sought to disguise it by persuading both antagonists to sign a meaningless pact pledging their "mutual desire for peace and unity." At a farewell dinner, guests heard a blandly smiling Mao propose a toast that seemed incredible to western ears in view of everything that had happened in the past eighteen years.

"Long live," Mao said politely, "Mr. Chiang Kai-shek!"

At that same moment KMT and Red forces were already clashing in eleven provinces. American planes were racing Nationalist troops to seize cities in the Yangtze valley, as well as in North China and Manchuria, with its vital industry and rail lines. Red forces led by Lin Piao were striking east and north from Yenan and North China by foot and packtrain.

The Russian Army now occupied Manchuria. Mao hoped that Stalin would agree to turn over to him the equipment and guns surrendered by the Japanese and permit the Chinese Red Army to entrench itself in the countryside before Chiang could claim the cities under the recent Sino-Soviet Treaty.

Upset over the looming civil war, Truman rushed General George Marshall to China with a new American proposal. If both sides would agree to establish a united and democratic China independent of Russia, the United States would provide huge amounts of financial, technical, and military aid.

Willing to make another try, Mao sent a delegation led by Chou En-lai to Chungking. In January, 1946, a cease-fire was announced, and both sides shook hands on an agreement to create a coalition government. But behind this surface harmony Mao and Chiang continued maneuvering for position, especially after it was learned that Stalin intended to pull his Soviet forces out of Manchuria by the end of April.

Marshall flew back to Washington to report his progress to Truman. Suddenly Chiang ordered his secret police in Mukden and Peking to arrest Communist members of the cease-fire teams in those cities. Mao struck back by ordering Lin Piao's troops to take over towns and villages from departing Soviet troops. A hundred savage skirmishes between both sides rapidly escalated into a full-scale civil war.

Marshall rushed back to China to repair the splintered agreement. Chiang now refused to listen. Mao was indignant because the American Congress had voted "all-out aid" to the Nationalists. He now suspected that the mediation efforts of both Hurley and Marshall had been undertaken primarily to stall the Chinese Red Army while Chiang consolidated his power. The Americans, Mao insisted coldly, must cease all military aid to Chiang and get all United States forces out of China.

Truman blamed both sides for forcing a civil war. "This is the way it goes," he declared. "Someone makes a proposal which is accepted by the other side with three qualifications. They are then accepted by the other side with three qualifications to each of the first three qualifications. It was an old Chinese way to be sure nothing would happen."

The Communists ended up in control of the major rural areas of central and northern China. The Kuomintang held the cities but were surrounded on all sides by the rapidly growing strength of the pro-Communist peasantry. Chiang was further chagrined to find that the cities he held in Manchuria were not prizes but empty shells. The Russians had stripped every factory of machinery before retreating.

As civil war flared throughout China, shopkeepers often hedged their bets prudently. A picture of Chiang Kai-shek hanging prominently on the wall usually had a picture of Mao Tse-tung on the reverse side for a quick flip-over when Red Army guerrillas took or raided a Nationalist town.

Chiang distressed his American military advisers by insisting that KMT troops dig in at the garrison rail junctions and cities they had occupied, in static defense postures. The Americans warned that he was pinning down his best divisions where Mao's guerrilla units could easily isolate them.

Despite Chiang's stubborn refusal to heed advice, Washington continued supporting him, unwilling to yield China to Communist power. By the end of June, 1946, the United States had equipped forty-five KMT divisions, trained 150,-000 KMT troops and counterrevolutionaries, and transported over half a million Nationalists in United States warships and aircraft. Some ninety thousand United States marines were landed in key Chinese cities to guard lines of communication for Chiang in northern China.

From the end of World War II through 1948 Chiang received almost seven billion dollars in American aid. It was hardly surprising that Mao Tse-tung now took a dim view of American foreign policy, seeing the United States as an imperialist enemy determined to crush him and the Chinese Revolution.

Foreign visitors making their way to Yenan in 1946 and 1947 found Mao still living and dressing with simple informality, a refreshing contrast to the sartorially immaculate and arrogant Chiang. Mao now ate less pepper, smoked fewer cigarettes, and retired earlier at night. He was growing heavier, but at fifty-four his hair was still thick, long, and black.

His greatest source of power was still his hold on the emotions of the Chinese peasantry. He urged them to stand fast against "the Nationalist oppressors," to make every sacrifice to cooperate with the Red Army, if they did not want this revolution to fail like futile peasant revolts of the past. Calling his crusade "the uninterrupted revolution," Mao warned the Chinese people that it might not be completed for a hundred years. For the sake of future generations they must have faith, patience, and—above all—perseverance.

His guerrillas fought brilliantly against odds of four to one. By the middle of 1947 enemy defeats and desertions, along with Red Army recruiting, had reduced the odds against Mao to two to one. In Nanking a frustrated Chiang sought to assure his disgusted American military advisers that his forces had now practically annihilated the Communists.

At the end of 1947, however, Mao accurately predicted the approaching end of Chiang Kai-shek's twenty-year dictatorship. The signs of an empire in decay were unmistakable in Nanking. Corruption and waste were worse than ever, along with a runaway inflation that was turning more millions of Chinese in Nationalist areas against the government.

When Chinese intellectuals urged reforms, Chiang indignantly outlawed their neutral Democratic League. They threw their influence and support behind Mao.

Chiang persisted in fighting positional warfare. He sent his divisions along railroads and highways to conquer cities and territory, using bombers, artillery, tanks, long supply lines, and frontal attacks. Mao's forces remained agile and flexible in mobile warfare. He never attempted to defend territory or cities. Evading pitched battles by swift retreats, he would then launch surprise attacks on Nationalist flanks and communications. KMT forces were never able to force decisive battles on the elusive Red Army.

In the areas Mao controlled he intensified land reform. His cadres slipped through North and Central China, promising land to landless peasants who joined the Red Army or cooperated with it. This prospect was irresistible for peasants whose indenture to landlords and moneylenders left them with only thirteen dollars a year income and who often had to survive on roots, cereal husks, and low-grade vegetables. The Red cadres promised all Chinese "absolute freedom of the press and absolute freedom of speech— except, of course, for enemies of the people."

Mao's revolution differed sharply from the one the Bolsheviks had made in 1917. It was a revolution from the bottom up rather than from the top down. It was fought in the countryside rather than in the cities. And the Red Army, rather than armed workers, were its spearhead. Not surprisingly, Mao felt that he owed little in the way of inspiration —let alone military help—to Moscow.

Stung, the Russians later accused Mao of having let hundreds of thousands of Red Army casualties die on the battlefields. Radio Moscow quoted Mao as having said that it was cheaper to recruit new men into the Red Army than to look after wounded soldiers. Perhaps these charges were true; certainly individual lives, compared to China's destiny, counted for little with Mao. But it seems unlikely that the Red Army would have fought so fiercely and loyally for Mao had his treatment of his men been so ruthless and cynical.

On the other hand there was documented evidence that the Nationalists shanghaied conscripts, marching them for up to four hundred miles roped together by their necks.

Often a bare 10 percent arrived at a KMT division area alive.

Mao persistently manifested his faith in men, not superior armaments, as decisive in warfare. In an interview with American journalist Anna Louise Strong, he said, "The atom bomb is a paper tiger which the U.S. reactionaries use to scare people. It . . . is a weapon of mass slaughter, but the outcome of a war is decided by the people, not by one or two new types of weapon. . . . Chiang Kai-shek and his supporters, the U.S. reactionaries, are all paper tigers, too."

He increasingly distrusted the Soviet Union as just another western nation, more sophisticated but driven by the same selfish nationalism. In Mao's eyes Stalinism had become an encrusted bureaucracy which had long since lost its revolutionary fervor and idealism. When Stalin sent Mao a Soviet text on partisan warfare, Mao tossed it to Liu Shao-ch'i. "Read this if you want to know what we ought to have done," he said dryly, "in order to end up dead."

With the war boom in the United States over, Mao foresaw a stock-market crash followed by a severe depression and revolution. "The American toiling masses have had enough of capitalist oppression and injustice," he declared.

Each day his radio station monitored American news broadcasts from San Francisco. When the news was given to him complete with stock-market quotations, he studied the market closely, looking for signs of a 1929-style collapse.

"When the next depression comes," he predicted confidently, "Americans will march on Washington and overthrow the Wall Street government. Then they'll establish a democratic regime that will cooperate with democratic forces all over the world, including the Red Chinese."

Mao's misjudgment of American affairs was underscored after he had read *Thunder out of China* by Theodore White and Annalee Jacoby. At first he was baffled that in the face of United States foreign policy an American book attacking Chiang would be printed by a capitalist publisher. Then he hit upon the solution: "The demand of the American toiling masses to know the truth about China *compelled* its publication!"

In the summer of 1948 Mao decided that it was time to mount a great counteroffensive against Chiang, challenging him decisively for the control of all China. Like the pieces of an enormous jigsaw puzzle springing into place, thousands of Red Army units in Manchuria suddenly emerged from hiding and joined into full divisions supported by captured tanks and artillery. They cut all railway lines and communications between Nationalist garrisons, isolating them in helpless pockets. In November, 1948, all Manchuria fell to the Communists.

When Mao began to repeat this strategy in North China, Nationalist garrisons were swept by panic. In a sixty-five-day battle at Soochow, Chiang lost six hundred thousand men. KMT troops now began surrendering first by thousands, then by full divisions, along with all their American equipment. Great numbers "changed hats"—joined the Red Army.

An alarmed Madame Chiang Kai-shek flew to America to make a desperate appeal for United States intervention to save her husband, but President Truman knew now that it was hopeless to try to prop up Chiang's dictatorship any longer and refused to throw away any more aid. He had no intention of letting American divisions become bogged down fighting an unwinnable ground war on the mainland of China.

Mao, with Manchuria and North China now in his hands, directed Lin Piao to encircle and cut off KMT garrisons in the Peking and Tientsin regions. Then the Red Army overran them one at a time. Tientsin was captured in January,

1949, after twenty-nine hours of fighting. Peking surrendered.

In a fierce battle near Hsuchow the Communists decimated Chiang's last good divisions. Now the warlords no longer obeyed the Generalissimo's commands, fleeing instead or "changing hats." The Communists poured southward, their ranks swelling with enlisted peasants, KMT deserters, and prisoners.

An urgent cable for Mao came from Moscow. Stalin asked him to be content with establishing a separate Red Chinese regime in the north. "If you press south," Stalin warned, "you may provoke the intervention of American imperialism."

Stalinists in the CCP Politburo agreed. Mao did not. "The revolution will not stop halfway," he vowed.

At the end of January, 1949, discredited and humiliated, Chiang Kai-shek was forced to resign as President. Mao was asked for terms. His reply was unequivocal: "Unconditional surrender!"

The Nationalists refused. Mao ordered a final big push. Commandeering thousands of small boats, Lin Piao crossed the opalistic Yangtze with his army and raced south in pursuit of the remnants of Chiang's divisions.

On April 23 they captured Nanking, the Nationalist capital. A jubilant Mao wrote:

> Around Mount Chung a sudden storm has arisen,
> A million courageous warriors cross the great river. . . .
> The universe is in turmoil, we are all exalted and resolute.
> Let us gather our courage and pursue the broken foe.

In May the Communists fought their way back into Shanghai, from which they had been driven by Chiang's 1927 massacre. On October 14 they drove the battered

Nationalists out of Canton. By the end of the year they were in triumphant occupation of the entire Chinese mainland.

With nowhere left to hide, Chiang Kai-shek and his aides fled to the offshore island of Formosa (Taiwan). There the fallen Generalissimo set up a "Republic of China" in exile.

Now, after four thousand years of emperors of every description, the Chinese people had something new—a Red emperor.

# Chapter 11

# China Awakes

*"Let China sleep. When it wakes, the world will be sorry."*
—Napoleon

*"They have awakened overnight from a sleep of thirty centuries and they will not go to sleep again."*
—André Malraux, *Man's Fate*

Many of the young Red Army warriors who marched through the captured cities were rustics awed by electricity and other urban wonders. Some vainly tried to light their cigarettes from light bulbs. Others mistook refrigerators for radios, and typewriters for transmitting sets.

Urban Chinese laughed at such innocents but were warmly impressed by their disciplined behavior, kindness toward civilians, and immunity to bribery. Many Red troops slept in the streets instead of turning people out of their homes. Here, obviously, was a different breed of soldier. They were welcomed everywhere with enthusiastic applause.

Mao was proud of his faith in them. Despite the sneers of Stalin and the Chinese Stalinists, he had politicized raw peasants into tough, dedicated troops who knew what they were fighting for and who were willing to endure any hardship or accept death to liberate their fellow countrymen.

After twenty years of struggle Mao's original ragged

handful of determined guerrillas, armed with homemade weapons, had become a force powerful enough to defeat a huge national army backed by the great might of the United States. Now their victory would begin changing China . . . and the world.

Not surprisingly, the engineer of so enormous a feat began to exhibit symptoms of self-intoxication. Had he not proved Marx, Lenin, and Stalin wrong in their view that the peasantry was incapable of independent political action and had to be led from above by an urban revolutionary elite?

Marx and the Russians, Mao now told his close friends, had known nothing about peasants and therefore even less about creating a revolution in a backward agricultural country. They had stressed the importance of developing a tight, rigid organization of city radicals. Mao had kept his revolutionary structure loose and agitated in the countryside to develop the will of the peasant masses to unite and rise.

Stalin had insisted that all revolutions must take their direction from Moscow, but his strategy had proved tragically wrong time after time. Mao had proved that Marxism worked in China only when it was changed to fit Chinese conditions. He had, moreover, proved wrong all the war colleges of the western nations that taught their military leaders that no irregulars could ever defeat a regular army in the long run. "When the poor are determined to fight," Mao declared firmly, "they are always victorious over the rich."

He had been right so many times, and the pro-Soviet faction in the CCP Politburo wrong so often, that he began to think of his ideas as incontrovertible dogma. Should not the words of a leader who had achieved the impossible become, for all Communists, a flawless blueprint for the future?

Mao was amused by the consternation in the United

States, where angry conservatives were now shrilly accusing the Truman administration of "giving China to the Communists." There was *some* truth to the charge, Mao laughed, but only because he had won largely with American arms captured from the Nationalists. The Red Army had also been helped by American-trained Nationalist officers and troops who had "changed hats."

As Cold War hysteria gripped the United States, relations rapidly chilled between Washington and Moscow. Despite Mao's rift with Stalin, he now saw an opportunity to mend fences in order to win badly needed Soviet economic aid for China. On April 10, 1949, he denounced American imperialism and vowed that if it provoked a third world war, Red China would support the Soviet Union. Hints came from the Kremlin of Stalin's willingness to let bygones be bygones.

Two months later Mao made an important policy speech, "On the People's Democratic Dictatorship," blueprinting his goals for the new China. It would be governed, he promised, by a popular front of peasants, workers, and petite bourgeoisie. All Chinese would enjoy the same rights except landlords and upper-class bourgeois linked to the Kuomintang.

Promising freedom of speech, assembly, association, and elections for people in the popular front, he added that the government would condone "suppression of antagonistic classes." His regime would be a "people's democratic dictatorship . . . democracy for the people, dictatorship for reactionaries."

There was no room in the new China, Mao warned, for fence-straddlers: "All Chinese without exception must lean either to the side of imperialism or to the side of socialism. Sitting on the fence will not do, nor is there a third road."

China's foreign policy, moreover, would be linked only with that of the Soviet Union: "Internationally, we belong to the anti-imperialist front, headed by the U.S.S.R. . . . We can look only to that front for genuine and friendly aid."

In September, 1949, he organized a Chinese People's Political Consultative Conference in Peking to ratify the new regime. Presiding at its opening, he declared proudly that China had finally "stood up" and would "never again be an insulted nation." Nine days later Chu Teh ended the conference with the cry "Long live Chairman Mao!"

On October 1, standing on the balcony of Peking's huge Gate of Heavenly Peace, Mao proclaimed the establishment of the People's Republic of China. Elected its first Chairman, he was now ruler of a fifth of the people on earth. For several nights there were celebrations and spontaneous dancing in the great square where public executions had taken place in the days of the Manchu dynasty.

Chou En-lai was named Mao's Premier and Foreign Minister. Because Lin Piao was now seriously ill, he retired from public affairs, later to return to Mao's side as Defense Minister.

Mao continued to dress as drably and plainly as when he had lived in the caves of Paoan and Yenan. But now his official residence was the splendid Palace of the People that rested on massive Egyptian pillars with lotus capitals painted red. Those granted audiences had to travel a polished corridor one hundred yards long to reach him.

Yet his manner remained as mild, gentle, and unassuming as ever as he received the ambassadors of Great Britain, the Soviet Union, Norway, the Netherlands, Sweden, Finland, and Switzerland as they presented their credentials to the new government. Conspicuously absent was the American ambassador, who had been pointedly recalled to Washington.

Mao's diplomatic behavior was so informal that once he received a lanky western diplomat by exclaiming with a smile, "My God—as tall as that!" Most diplomats and journalists found the new "Red emperor" charming and intelligent.

In the United States, meanwhile, the humiliating failure of American foreign policy in China compelled the Truman administration to issue a white paper defending itself against Republican charges of having caused Chiang's downfall. The white paper finally revealed to Americans what General Stilwell had not been allowed to tell them— that Chiang had ruined himself by his reactionary rule, corrupt regime, and stubborn refusal to heed his American advisers.

The white paper also carried a veiled warning to Mao not to move closer to Moscow. Secretary of State Dean Acheson made it clear that if he did, the United States would become actively hostile, even to the point of using armed forces.

Mao reacted angrily by writing in the Chinese press five bitter attacks on America's Asian policies. He suggested, however, that a "very close friendship" between the American and Chinese *people* was possible, despite "reactionaries" in the United States. This early gesture to Americans over the heads of their government was a theme he would return to twenty-two years later, when he introduced his "Ping-Pong diplomacy."

Mao's most pressing problem was restoring the country's shattered economy. There was no money in the treasury. Half of China's meager industry had been destroyed in the fighting. The railroads were unusable because of bombing or disrepair. Many regions of China faced hunger. Even at the best of times, life expectancy for Chinese men had been only thirty-two years and for women thirty-four years, compared to sixty-six and seventy-two years for Americans.

So two months after proclaiming his People's Republic, Mao went to Moscow to seek help. It was the first time in his life that he had been outside of China's borders.

Stalin received him coolly but civilly. After two months of hard bargaining Mao could obtain only a five-year three-hundred-million-dollar loan—a tenth of the aid he asked for. And Stalin's price came high. Mao was forced to recognize the "independence" of Outer Mongolia, where many Chinese had settled. Moreover, he was compelled to let Soviet agents occupy strategic positions in the government, from which they could influence Chinese policy and serve as Kremlin spies.

But the Sino-Soviet Treaty of Alliance signed in February, 1950, gave Mao 50,000 engineers, technicians, and scientists to help build aircraft, automobile, and other plants. Along with the sophisticated weaponry Stalin gave him went 2,500 military advisers to train the Red Army in their use. Thousands of Chinese were given technical training of all kinds in Soviet plants and laboratories.

The treaty also called for mutual military assistance in case of attack by Japan "or any state allied with it," an obvious reference to the United States. In Yugoslavia Marshal Tito blamed Washington for driving Mao into Russian hands, pointing out that if Mao had been offered American aid without strings, he would have become an anti-Kremlin Tito of the Far East.

Returning home, Mao began to purge the corrupt old China he had inherited to purify it for the great changes coming. He proved as ruthless as Stalin in liquidating former Kuomintang bureaucrats and army officers, as well as landlords and other "class enemies." Great numbers of people were seized and thrown into prison. Village temples, churches, and halls overflowed with arrested Chinese waiting to be tried by "revolutionary people's courts" in the village squares.

Communist cadres would read out charges against the accused, invite testimony documenting their offenses, then ask the people what should be done with them. By the tens of thousands, landlords and officials who had beaten and killed peasants were executed on the spot.

Landlords were forced to kneel and surrender title deeds to their lands, which were then burned and their lands awarded to tenant farmers who worked on them. Landlords who had charged exorbitant rents were tortured until they agreed to pay back cheated tenants in full.

Mao saw these revolutionary trials, reminiscent of the French Reign of Terror, as valuable in convincing the peasantry that things really had changed in China. The "bad old days" were over, and the masses were now the rulers.

In their zeal to purge the old guard, Communist cadres encouraged young people to denounce anti-Maoist members of their own families. The older generation was horrified at this violation of the old Chinese tradition of filial respect and obedience. But Mao warned in a speech that his victory of arms had been only "the first step in a long march." He now intended to shake the nation awake from its Confucian slumber, dragging its people forcefully out of the Middle Ages into the twentieth century.

To set an example of simple, thrifty living, Mao moved out of the huge palace in Peking and took up residence in a little lakeshore villa. Imposing price control to end inflation, he stabilized the Chinese currency. Corrupt public officials found themselves fired and replaced by scrupulously honest party members.

Energetic medical campaigns fought and wiped out cholera and smallpox. Hospital construction went up all over China at the rate of two a week. Cleanliness campaigns persuaded urban and village dwellers to clean up the streets themselves. Expensive funeral rites were held up to ridicule while inexpensive cremations were encouraged as "more civilized."

To transform existing social relationships out of their Confucian framework, Mao passed a marriage law in April, 1950, that established equal rights for women. Ending the "whole feudal system" of marriage and family life, he broke the power of parents over children by giving women free choice of marriage partners and the right to protest against unreasonable interference by mothers-in-law. The Marriage Law also established equal status for wives and husbands in the home, legal status for all children born out of wedlock, and the right of divorce when mutually agreed upon by both husband and wife.

Mao took pride in the fact that the Marriage Law made China more "modern and advanced" than many of the western nations. Passing the law was one thing, however; getting every Chinese family to observe it was another. Mao's attack on the old ways of family life met with stubborn resistance, and change in this sphere of the new China was slow.

He began demobilizing the Red Army for economy and at the same time gained more hands for farms and factories. In a speech on June 23, 1950, he explained that they now needed only to win the struggle against poverty, because "the trial of war already belongs basically to the past."

Two days later North Korean troops invaded South Korea, as part of a vast Cold War chess game being played between Moscow and Washington. Stalin saw the American satellite of South Korea as a threat to Russia's back door. He manipulated his own satellite of North Korea against it, seeking, without direct Soviet involvement, to get all American military bases off the Asian mainland.

It was clear that Stalin had not consulted Mao before making this move. Irked, Mao had no intention of getting involved. He was not eager to see all of Korea become a Moscow satellite, putting China deeper inside a Soviet nutcracker. Moreover, it was Formosa, not Korea, that preoccupied Mao as a threat. Chiang Kai-shek kept boasting of his intention to invade the mainland and retake China.

Mao was highly suspicious when President Truman "neutralized" the Taiwan Strait by deploying the United States Seventh Fleet off the China coast. Speeding Red Army units to Fukien Province opposite Formosa, Mao angrily called upon the Chinese people to be ready to "defeat any provocation by U.S. imperialism." Washington charged Mao with planning to invade Formosa and liquidate Chiang's rival government.

Meanwhile the Korean War had developed into large-scale fighting by Soviet-armed North Koreans against American-armed South Koreans, aided by a United Nations army led by General Douglas MacArthur that consisted mainly of American forces. Mao watched uneasily as MacArthur spearheaded his infantry and air assaults toward the Yalu River on the Manchurian border.

The United Nations assured Peking that this frontier would not be crossed, but Mao suspected a western plot against him. In 1918 England, France, and the United States had joined forces to invade Siberia, trying to overthrow the newly established Soviet Union. Why wouldn't they try the same thing now against a new Red China, using North Korea as an air base and corridor through which to channel an invasion?

Strong pressure came from Stalin to prevent the rout of North Korean forces by MacArthur. Did Mao, Moscow pointed out, want American air bases on his northern border? Stalin offered to arm and supply all Chinese "volunteers" Mao sent across the Yalu to counterattack the Americans. Not only that, but Moscow was willing to give China large-scale economic aid.

Stalin's supporters in the CCP Politburo added their pressure on Mao. Finally he reluctantly agreed. But he was determined not to pull Stalin's chestnuts out of the fire for him. If China saved North Korea, it would be Chinese, not Soviet, influence that prevailed there afterward.

On May 30, 1951, advance elements of Mao's Fourth Field Army of almost a quarter of a million men began to cross the Yalu at night, disappearing silently into the rugged mountains of North Korea. Two days later General MacArthur met with President Truman at Wake Island to reassure him that according to all United States Intelligence reports, the Chinese could not, and would not, cross the Yalu in force.

At a Senate hearing later Senator Leverett Saltonstall asked the Secretary of State, "They really fooled us when it comes right down to it, didn't they?"

"Yes, sir," admitted Dean Acheson.

With Moscow footing the bill for the Chinese "volunteers to aid North Korea," Mao had no need to put China on a wartime basis. While the struggle in Korea seesawed back and forth, he returned his attention to domestic problems.

Some members of the CCP Politburo were angered by a wave of complaints in the cities, among the bourgeois, intellectuals, and Stalinist officials, against the brutal slaughter practiced in the land-reform program. Mao was being accused of responsibility for the unnecessary deaths of millions of non-Communists. A few of his followers urged him to order the execution of his chief critics.

"A head isn't a leek," he reproached them mildly. "Once it's been cut, it doesn't grow again." Instead he organized a campaign against "counterrevolutionary elements." Grumbling peasants and workers were to be "educated and convinced." Landlords and officials would be "forced to transform themselves through labor in order to become new people." Dissent quickly died away.

Although Mao may have preferred converting the mass of his opponents, there is little doubt that he was responsible for the tactics of his cadres in whipping up peasants into a murderous fury against landlords and former KMT officials. He had, after all, the example of Stalin, who had massacred—by Stalin's own admission—no less than ten million Russian kulaks to enforce Soviet collectivization.

It was paradoxical in Mao that he seemed capable of generosity toward enemy soldiers, because he saw them as simply misled workers and peasants, and toward political rivals he regarded as misled comrades. It meant far more to him to win them over to his side than to see them dead. But when his plans were opposed by an impersonal, faceless mass he identified only as "rich landlords, corrupt bureaucrats and imperialist lackeys"—class enemies—he was often filled with a murderous rage that led to great bloodshed.

While he maintained his façade of modesty, it became increasingly obvious that he was encouraging a personality cult. In 1951 a book appeared with the title *Songs to the Glory of Mao Tse-tung.* A new collection of his speeches and writings was issued, with all party cadres, schools, and universities ordered to encourage study of "Mao Tse-tung's thought."

One sycophantic aide went for a swim with Mao in the Yangtze River and afterward gushed in print: "The Chairman's energy, his robust frame, made me think of the rising sun. I murmured to myself, 'Let thy life be long and thy health perfect.' Finding myself close to the Chairman, the mightiest waves lost their terror for me." That Mao could encourage, or even tolerate, such fawning flattery suggested that he had now lost all semblance of a sense of humor.

More and more his decrees began to resemble those of the ancient Chinese emperors who had sought to isolate their people from the rest of the world behind the Great Wall. Mao's wall consisted of propaganda posters, a one-party press, agit-prop theater, songs to glorify Chairman

Mao and his thought, and punishment of dissent as political heresy. All Chinese must think as he did and work in unison to translate his ideas into reality as quickly as possible. How else could Mao bring them into the promised land of socialism before death took him from his people?

# Chapter 12

# "Conflict with China Is Inevitable"

In March, 1953, Mao was stunned by a sudden announcement from the Kremlin. Joseph Stalin was dead.

In a tribute that appeared in *Pravda* Mao hailed the late dictator as "the greatest genius of the present age." He added, "Today we have lost a great teacher and a most sincere friend. . . . It is impossible to express in words the grief which this misfortune has evoked. . . . On questions of the Chinese Revolution he displayed the greatest wisdom."

Some CCP Politburo members laughed in private, taking Mao's extravagant panegyric as straight-faced irony meant to satisfy protocol while being an "inside" joke for those who knew better, but Chinese Stalinists took Mao's tribute at face value. After all, they reasoned, Mao had grown up in Joseph Stalin's great shadow, and it was natural that Stalin's death should have a traumatic effect upon him.

Stalin's passing from the scene gave the new American President, Dwight D. Eisenhower, hope that it now might be possible to arrange a truce in the fruitless Korean War. By this time the war had struck home to Mao personally. His surviving son by his first wife had been killed in combat with the Chinese "volunteers." Through Chou En-lai Mao proposed to Soviet Foreign Minister Vyacheslav Molotov a plan for the exchange of sick and wounded prisoners. Molotov approved this first step toward ending the Korean War on April 1, 1953.

The rise of Nikita Khrushchev to power in place of Joseph Stalin had a profound influence on the course of world events. Unlike Stalin, Khrushchev was convinced that the best interests of the Soviet Union would now be served not by continuing the Cold War with the United States, but by a new policy of "coexistence." Then Russia could devote its treasure and energy to economic growth instead of sterile conflict.

In September, 1953, the Russians sought to win Mao over to this new policy by offering to build ninety-one new factories in China and signing an agreement to this effect. Mao launched a Five-Year Plan aimed primarily at industrializing his country. The results were impressive.

In just three years five hundred new factories were built, a third of them with Russian aid. Mining, agriculture, electric power, and road and rail construction were expanded dramatically. War-damaged dikes against flood were completely rebuilt. By the end of the Five-Year Plan Mao had more than doubled the industrial production of his country.

Chinese businessmen who failed to support this program by buying sufficient government bonds were heavily fined. Many had their businesses confiscated by the state, which retained the former owners as salaried managers. Mao steadily nationalized private business in China by firing "sugar-coated bullets"—campaigns to "correct" speculation, tax evasion, bribery, fraud, waste, and corruption by putting enterprises accused of such malpractice under state control.

Despite the extensive Soviet help he was now receiving, Mao turned a deaf ear to the Russians' plea that he do nothing to make waves and stir up anti-Communist feeling in Washington. For one thing, Mao now frankly enjoyed playing games with the Americans and alarming them by military feints.

In 1954 he began bombarding the offshore islands of Quemoy and Matsu, on which Chiang Kai-shek had garrisoned large numbers of Nationalist troops. The Pentagon, fearful of a Red Chinese attempt to invade Formosa, rushed reinforcements to join the Seventh Fleet in the Taiwan Strait. Mao admitted to correspondent Edgar Snow that it amused him to make "a loud noise" in order to stampede the mighty American navy into rushing here and there in response to his gambits.

Eisenhower's Secretary of State, John Foster Dulles, wanted to blockade Red China with a clear-cut warning that the United States would fight to defend the offshore islands. "Before this problem is solved," he said, "I believe there is at least an even chance that the United States will have to go to war." The President, however, aware that historically the islands belonged to mainland China, saw no sense in risking a major war in Asia, without allies, for so dubious a cause.

Mao was not intimidated by Dulles's saber-rattling. He was convinced that the American people would never have the patience of the Chinese to wait out a prolonged struggle. "A Communist war which lasts ten years may be surprising to other countries," he was quoted by *Time* magazine, "but for us this is only the preface."

In the fall of 1954 Khrushchev paid an unexpected visit to Peking to see Mao and woo him into supporting the coexistence policy. Putting his best foot forward, the Soviet leader offered to end Moscow's "special rights" in China, providing new economic assistance as well. Mao was cordial, promised full support for Soviet policies, and acknowledged Moscow as "leader of the Communist world." Never had Sino-Soviet relations seemed so harmonious. Yet secretly each Communist leader deeply distrusted the other.

"I remember when I came back from China in 1954," Khrushchev later recalled, "I told my comrades: 'Conflict with China is inevitable.' During my visit to Peking Mao and I used to lie around the swimming pool, chatting like the best old friends. But it was all too sickeningly sweet. I was never exactly sure I understood what Mao meant."

With Stalin dead, Mao felt that he was now the senior Communist leader on the world scene and need no longer defer to Moscow. He was also extremely skeptical of Khrushchev's confidence that an accommodation could be reached with the capitalist world. Khrushchev was a "revisionist" who was betraying the principles of Marx by pursuing an illusion that the capitalist West would stand idly by and let communism demonstrate a better way of life for the world's toilers.

Mao was also leery of the challenge of India's Jawaharlal Nehru for the leadership of Asia. He privately scorned Nehru as a weak apologist for western democracy. When Nehru visited Peking in 1954, he warned Mao against provoking a nuclear war against Asia by the West, which would end in the annihilation of all mankind. Mao shrugged contemptuously.

"If the worst came to the worst and half of mankind died," he replied, "the other half would still remain. Imperialism would be razed to the ground, and the whole world would become socialist. In a number of years there would again be twenty-seven hundred million people and probably more."

Alarmed, Nehru disagreed emphatically. From his knowledge as chairman of India's Atomic Energy Commission he warned Mao that no nation subjected to nuclear attack could survive.

"Governments might disappear," Mao conceded indifferently, "but others would soon arise to replace them."

A worried Nehru helped organize the Bandung Conference of twenty-nine Asian-African nations in April, 1955, to muster the world's neutral leaders against the threat of nuclear disaster. Mao's delegates sought to form an anti-imperialist alliance against the NATO and SEATO nations. Failing, they reluctantly signed the conference's call for peaceful coexistence.

Mao was far less disturbed about nuclear weapons than by the failure of two thirds of China's peasants to join collective farms. In 1955 he sought to force collectivization by denying holdouts fertilizer, water from communal irrigation ditches, and help at harvesttime.

The Twentieth Communist Party Congress in Moscow in 1956 brought a new development that shook Mao to the core. In an address that also astounded the world Khrushchev suddenly denounced the late Joseph Stalin as a monstrous dictator and attacked the personality cult that Stalin had built as idolatry.

Mao was furious at Khrushchev for having taken this historic step without consulting him. Khrushchev's charges had thrown into doubt the credibility of the Communist line during the three whole decades it had been shaped by Stalin. Mao also felt icy contempt for Stalin's former henchman who, like a spiteful cur, now snapped at the heels of a brutal dead master who could no longer kick him.

"In what position does Khrushchev," Mao asked scornfully, "who participated in the leadership of the party and the state during Stalin's period, place himself when he beats his breast, pounds the table and shouts abuse of Stalin at the top of his voice? In the position of an accomplice to a 'murderer' or 'bandit'? Or in the same position as a 'fool' or 'idiot'?"

Mao was also incensed because Khrushchev's attack on Stalin for building a personality cult could just as well apply to Mao. If Stalin could be condemned as an egomaniac, then so, obviously, could Mao. Even more serious, if all of Stalin's accomplishments for Russia could be buried and forgotten under an avalanche of condemnation for his crimes and blunders, then why could not some Chinese Khrushchev one day destroy Mao's place in history with the same one-sided attack?

"Some people consider that Stalin was wrong in everything," observed an editorial in the Peking *People's Daily* either written or inspired by Mao. "This is a grave misconception. Stalin was a great Marxist-Leninist . . . who committed several gross errors without realizing that they were errors. We should view Stalin from an historical standpoint . . . to see where he was right and where he was wrong, and draw useful lessons." This view was later adopted by the Kremlin itself.

Mao also moved to protect himself against any unpleasant fallout from Khrushchev's exposure of Stalin. The CCP Politburo explained to the Chinese people that the Russian leader's attack had been directed against Stalin personally, not against the Communist system, and also had nothing to do with China because Chairman Mao had always pursued a course independent of both Stalin and the Comintern.

The end of that same year brought another surprise for Mao. Khrushchev reverted to Stalinism himself by using Soviet tank forces to put down a popular uprising in Moscow's satellite, Hungary. World indignation shook the Kremlin, and other Soviet satellites in Eastern Europe were furious.

Khrushchev appealed to Mao for moral support. Putting the Soviet leader in his debt, Mao sent Prime Minister Chou En-lai to speak in Moscow, Warsaw, and Budapest, defending the Soviet action in Hungary as necessary to thwart a western-supported plot to restore capitalism.

Mao grew uneasy about Hungary's portents for his own regime. By his own estimate no fewer than eight hundred thousand opponents of Maoism had been eliminated forcibly between 1949 and 1954 before terror tactics had been replaced by a program of "persuasion and education." Was there, perhaps, still enough underground resentment in China that, given a spark, might explode into anti-Communist riots like those in Budapest?

He decided it might be wiser to reduce any pressure in the Chinese boiler by letting off steam. Opponents of his regime would be encouraged to express constructive criticism openly, pointing the way to useful reforms.

In February, 1957, he delivered his famous speech, "On the Correct Handling of Contradictions among People." It was certainly possible for socialist citizens to disagree, Mao declared, and it was best to have all contradictory views aired. "In every field let one hundred flowers blossom," he urged, "and let one hundred schools of thought contend."

The country's intellectuals, and especially the young, were astonished at being urged to speak out critically in the press and open forums against whatever they found wrong. In Moscow Khrushchev, reading the speech incredulously, thought that Mao must have taken leave of his senses. C.B.S. correspondent Daniel Schorr asked the Soviet leader whether similar conflicting views also existed in the Soviet Union.

"We believe," Khrushchev replied brusquely, "that we have no contradictions of that nature."

Chinese intellectuals were quick to take advantage of their new opportunity. Many began to make sharp attacks on the CCP. "The Communist party does not represent the people's interests," one critic charged in the press. "It only represents the interests of the party." A girl student at the People's University in Peking denounced 80 percent of the CCP as reactionaries who kept China tied to Soviet policy, whereas Chairman Mao wanted to follow an independent Communist course like Tito.

Other critics objected to the Maoist personality cult, comparing it to Stalin's. The hundred flowers Mao had asked for multiplied to thousands, blooming with ever-increasing audacity. Shrill, emotional arguments led to public brawls.

Mao was stunned. He had expected constructive and polite criticism, but instead he and the CCP were being drenched under a tidal wave of political opposition. His comrades urged Mao to put a stop to the Hundred Flowers Campaign before it spread disaffection throughout the country, provoking uprisings.

Mao grimly decided that China's intellectuals needed serious "reeducation" in Marxism-Leninism. He canceled the Hundred Flowers program, admitting that it had been a failure. The writings and speeches of all intellectuals were scrutinized carefully by party cadres for signs of disaffection.

Those who had dared speak out against the regime were ordered to "corrective labor." One professor had to clean the lavatories of the university where he had taught. Intellectuals were pressured to confess "sins of pride."

Mathematicians confessed that they had worked with pure math only, instead of practical math problems that could help the country, for fear they would be accused by colleagues of vulgarizing their talents. Officials who had opposed Mao's land-reform program admitted that they had discovered their error by studying Mao's thoughts and acquiring a "whole new understanding." Those whose public repentance seemed sincere were declared "rehabilitated" and left in place.

Meanwhile fresh truculence on the part of the American Secretary of State forced Mao's attention back to foreign affairs. Dulles, convinced that communism on the Chinese mainland was only a temporary "aberration," was determined to do all he could short of a shooting war to overturn it. "We owe it to ourselves, our allies, and the Chinese people," he announced sanctimoniously, "to contribute to that passing." He branded Red China an aggressive menace to world peace.

Mao fired back a refutation. The United States had planes and troops in bases all over the world; China had none. Every sixteen days America spent in armaments what China appropriated for a whole year. Well over half of America's budget went to the military, compared to only 8 percent of China's. Which nation, then, was the *real* threat to world peace?

"We stand firmly for peace and against war," Mao vowed. "But if the imperialists insist on unleashing another war, we should not be afraid of it. . . .We should also unite with their people in striving to coexist in peace, do business together and prevent any possible war, but definitely should not harbor any unrealistic notions about those countries."

In the summer of 1957 Khrushchev sought to woo Mao fully back into the Soviet camp by acknowledging that he had always been right in pursuing his own version of communism. "China follows a Marxist path in her own Chinese way," he declared, "but that is no cause for quarrel. China is a large, original country. She does not copy anything. Differing ways to socialism are only tributaries to the mainstream."

Mao, his point won at last, was flattered and mollified, but he only began to move closer to Moscow when the Russians demonstrated that they were well ahead of the United States in the nuclear-arms race. In October, 1957, only three months after developing an intercontinental ballistic missile (ICBM), Soviet scientists launched the first man-made satellite, *Sputnik I*, into a space orbit around the earth.

This achievement stunned and frightened the Pentagon; satellites could carry nuclear warheads. Mao, too, was greatly impressed. "The east wind," he declared in satisfaction, "prevails over the west wind."

He led a delegation to Moscow in November, his second and last visit. As part of a new Sino-Soviet trade pact, Khrushchev agreed to help China manufacture its own nuclear weapons. His reward came when Mao stayed on to address an important Moscow conference of world Communist leaders.

"The socialist camp must have a head," Mao now acknowledged, "and this head is the U.S.S.R." He told the delegates that "war maniacs might drop atomic and hydrogen bombs everywhere," but that no socialist country would ever initiate nuclear warfare. The Russians enthusiastically applauded Mao's new endorsement of their coexistence policy, but their smiles froze as Mao repeated what he had told Nehru about building socialism with half the world's population if the other half was destroyed in a nuclear holocaust.

"We Chinese have not yet completed our construction, and we desire peace," Mao added. "However, if imperialism insists on fighting a war, we will have no alternative but . . . to fight to the finish before going ahead with our construction. If you remain in daily fear of war, and war eventually comes, what will you do then?"

When Mao had returned to China, a nervous Khrushchev began to have second thoughts about putting nuclear weapons in the hands of a firebrand like Mao Tse-tung. He had promised Mao a sample atomic bomb and technical data on its manufacture. Now he sent Peking only limited nuclear information that would take Chinese scientists far longer to utilize successfully. Sino-Soviet relations cooled rapidly.

By January, 1958, Mao was once more taking wry potshots at the Russians and his pro-Soviet comrades in the CCP: "Some people have suggested that if our comrades, the Soviet advisers, see we are not copying from them, they will complain or be discontented. Well, I might ask these Soviet comrades, 'Are you copying from China? . . . If you don't copy from us, we won't copy from you either!' "

The truth was that there was little in Chinese economic development that was worth copying. Mao was in trouble. His attempt to industrialize the country hastily, without prudent coordination of labor, materials, and priorities, had now resulted in half-finished and abandoned buildings everywhere. Taking peasants off farms for construction work and bungling in the land-reform program had left China with only two thirds of the food needed to eliminate famine.

The trouble, Mao decided, was a failure of national will-power. The people needed to be infused with the same indomitable spirit that had animated the heroic survivors of the Long March. Once inspired, they would take a convulsive "great leap forward" that would galvanize *all* production, in both farms and factories, to record levels!

"Our low living standards," later explained Yung Lung-kuei, a prominent Chinese economist, "called for a great push in production. This was the desire of the broad masses of the people, who wanted to see China transformed into a prosperous country. Thus was the Great Leap Forward inspired, and the masses threw themselves into the task with resolution."

To solve China's staggering array of problems by a mass application of willpower and manpower, Mao raised a new slogan: "Twenty years in a day!" All Chinese were urged to find shortcuts to double their work in half the time. Supervisors and technicians who protested that such speed-ups were ruinous or impossible were fired. Farms were collectivized at top speed and operated at a frenzied pace. Peasants attempted to turn out quality steel in backyard furnaces. The Ming Tombs dam was built in record time by the hand labor of fifty thousand workers rushing around like a colony of ants.

The *People's Daily* made it clear that being Red was now

far more important than being expert. "Medical education needs reforming," it editorialized. "There is altogether no need to read so many books. How long did it take Hua T'o [the father of Chinese medicine] to learn what he knew?" Chinese doctors were ordered to discover a cancer cure within five years. The paper also called for the swift education of nuclear physicists: "The pursuit of atomic science is not the privilege of a select few, and it does not require long training; it can be carried out in wide circles in a short time."

Mao himself went into the countryside to encourage the formation of experimental "people's communes" that substituted hand labor for scarce agricultural machinery. "There is no such thing as poor land," he assured peasants. "There are only poor methods of cultivating the land. It is possible to modify all natural conditions, if people demonstrate fully their capacities for action." He offered them a hopeful new slogan to raise their spirits: "Three years of suffering, and a thousand years of happiness!" By the end of three years, he promised, every Chinese could have 1,-600 pounds of food grains and 110 pounds of pork annually. He later cited the same goals to visiting Field Marshal Bernard Montgomery but admitted candidly that he did not expect China to achieve them for another fifty years.

Peasants and workers were continually urged, "Forward! Follow 100 percent, and without the slightest reservation, the way of Mao Tse-tung!" At first, to Mao's delight, the Great Leap Forward appeared to be working. Eager-to-please officials published figures of economic achievement that exaggerated actual production by 40 to 50 percent.

It rapidly grew apparent, however, that the Great Leap Forward had been a disastrous failure. In many provinces the land was lying fallow because peasants drafted to build roads, dams, and factories had no time to work it. Unwise haste had made waste in fields and factories. Chinese working as hard as they could were outraged by new impossible quotas imposed as a result of their officials' falsified statistics.

Peasant passive resistance was causing the commune system to break down. Thousands were under "military discipline" for balking at the collectivization of their daily lives and routines, from weddings and baths to funerals and haircuts.

Mao, a peasant's son, had forgotten the stubborn individuality of the Chinese peasant. It had been a miscalculation to think he could transform such men of the soil into agrarian robots simply because he had been able to make good guerrilla fighters out of them. Even the old emperors of China had never interfered with the rights of the peasants to do their own sowing and reaping. Now Mao had lost their confidence by forcing them to work on collectives.

His mistake was the signal for all his old enemies once more to begin sharpening their knives. Their attacks were not long in coming.

# Chapter 13

# The Great Leap
# Forward Stumbles

Mao had erred, his political rivals in the CCP Politburo said accusingly, by persisting in his policy of building the revolution on the peasantry, instead of concentrating on developing heavy industry. The Great Leap Forward had produced neither humming factories nor bumper harvests, but only widespread disillusionment, dissatisfaction, and hunger.

Mao admitted that there were serious problems but vowed, "The people are now stirring; there is a fervent tide. Our nation is like an atom. After the atom's nuclear fission, the thermal energy released will be so formidable that we will be able to accomplish all that we now cannot do!"

His opponents voiced sharp criticism of Mao's running feud with Khrushchev, who had just called for a summit meeting of the United States, Britain, France, India, and the Soviet Union to settle a crisis in the Middle East. Khrushchev's flirtations with the West, they warned, might end in a U.S.–U.S.S.R. alliance and a China isolated from the rest of the world.

When Khrushchev visited Peking, Mao protested bitterly against his dealings with "American imperialists" who were still backing Chiang Kai-shek on Formosa. Khrushchev placated Mao by withdrawing his proposal for a summit meeting.

To set the Russian leader an example of how to deal with imperialists, in August, 1958, Mao ordered the resumption of shelling of the offshore islands. Dulles rushed troops, marines, and planes to strengthen the Seventh Fleet and once more hinted darkly that Mao might be courting nuclear disaster.

"American imperialism is nothing but a paper tiger," Mao scoffed again. And he added coolly, "The east wind prevails over the west wind more and more every day."

Worried, Khrushchev warned Eisenhower that any attack on Red China would compel Moscow, by treaty, to go to the aid of Mao. The President restrained Dulles, then compelled Chiang Kai-shek to join with Washington in assuring Mao that the Nationalists would not try to invade the mainland.

Mao's response to this concession was whimsical. He let Nationalist ships bring supplies to Quemoy and Matsu on even-numbered days and shelled them on odd-numbered days. Baffled by the "inscrutable Oriental mind," Eisenhower later sighed, "I wondered if we were in a Gilbert and Sullivan war!"

Khrushchev became increasingly irked with Mao for stirring up trouble with Washington. And he was angry at Mao's refusal to listen to Soviet advisers, who had warned against the Great Leap Forward. Moscow now began withdrawing all nuclear assistance, recalling technicians, and sharply reducing Chinese aid and trade.

In a conversation with Senator Hubert Humphrey on December 1, 1958, Khrushchev derided Mao's commune plan as old-fashioned and reactionary. "You can't get production without offering incentives," he criticized. And at the Twenty-first Soviet Congress he scoffed, "It's impossible to *leap* into communism."

Chen Shao-yu, former head of the CCP who was permanent Chinese delegate to the revived Comintern (now called the Cominform), created a sensation by denouncing Mao. The Chairman, Chen accused, had betrayed Marxism-Leninism, organized a "pseudo-Communist party," sought to set up his own Maoist international, operated a dictatorship based on military terror, disbanded the workers' union, liquidated intellectuals, and—most horrendous of all—had deliberately sought to provoke nuclear warfare between the United States and the Soviet Union. This blast from the Cominform, added to Mao's loss of prestige because of the failure of the Great Leap Forward, created a strong wave of discontent with his leadership among the party faithful in Peking.

Peng Teh-huai, the Minister of Defense, formed a new anti-Mao bloc within the CCP Politburo. It received tacit support from Prime Minister Chou En-lai, insofar as the anti-Maoists sought to abandon the Great Leap and return to more moderate, rational policies.

There was a showdown meeting of the Politburo. "One can't be rash," Mao now conceded. "There must be a step-by-step process. In eating meat, one can only consume one piece at a time. One can never hope to become a 'fatso' at one stroke." Pointing a now-plump finger at Marshal Chu Teh, Mao smiled, "The Commander in Chief and I didn't get this fat in a single day."

He defended the Great Leap, however, as a sound plan that had been ruined by improper execution by the party cadres. They had also failed to arouse sufficient revolutionary enthusiasm among the masses. And Mao complained of the lack of support from China's intellectuals. "The intellectual thinks only of a more comfortable life," he said bitterly, "when his mind should be on the revolution."

As a veteran guerrilla fighter, though, Mao knew better than to press a losing battle. In a strategic retreat he told the

Politburo that he had decided not to stand as a candidate for another four-year term as President of the Chinese People's Republic. "I am going to retire to make further studies of Marxism and Leninism, to meditate on the doctrine," he declared, adding that he planned to withdraw from all active politics and day-to-day administration.

Peng Teh-huai's faction won the election of Liu Shao-ch'i as President in place of Mao. At the same time Mao did not offer to surrender his key position of behind-the-scenes power as Chairman of the CCP, and none in the Politburo dared attempt to strip him of it.

Mao burned with secret rage at the "treachery" of those in the Politburo who had failed to support him. He began referring to them as "women with bound feet" and "capitalist-roaders" who had betrayed both him and the revolution.

"Mao has retired to his room," reported one British correspondent, "and slammed the door on the world."

He spent that winter in Hangkow in a large, simple house at the foot of a mountain, reading and reflecting among flowering shrubs frequented by blue-winged sand martins, tanagers, and hummingbirds. He also took trips through the provinces of central and southern China to inspect village communes and city factories and find out what had gone wrong.

The party cadres, who were the on-the-spot local power in China, told him. The Great Leap Forward had been a wholly impractical program that had almost wrecked the economy of their local districts. Worst of all, they pointed out, had been the serious underestimate of transport needs. Delayed deliveries of raw materials, spare parts, machinery, and agricultural products had idled plants and communes for weeks at a time.

Depressed, Mao was made even more gloomy by a famine stemming from the bungling of the Great Leap, aggravated by severe droughts and floods. In July, 1959, he made a surprisingly humble speech taking the blame on his own shoulders.

"Coal and iron cannot walk by themselves," he sighed. "They must be transported. This point I had not considered adequately. . . . Prior to August of last year I devoted most of my energy to the revolutionary side of things. I am fundamentally incompetent on economic construction, and I do not understand industrial planning."

The speech was greeted with great astonishment and no little admiration for its candor. For a leader who had tried to persuade his people that his ideas about everything were infallible, it was a humiliating confession of error. But Mao was also proving that he practiced what he preached—that only by honest public confession of one's mistakes could one expiate them and learn from them.

He was now devoting himself increasingly to foreign affairs, feeling more comfortable in the role of defender of the nation. It was in the field of military strategy, after all, that he had proved his genius.

He received a series of foreign dignitaries for private talks. Field Marshal Montgomery visited him in May, 1959, and said afterward, "Mao is a very delightful person to meet and talk with. He may be a Communist. That is his business. But he did not give me any indication that he is planning to force his ideology down the throats of any other nation, or that he plans to communize the world. . . . Like all sons of the soil, he is a genuine democrat."

Former French Cabinet Minister François Mitterand was not quite that euphoric after his visit to Peking. "Mao is a humanist for whom wisdom and culture acquire meaning when identified with action," Mitterand observed cautiously. "He escapes all ordinary definitions."

As though to prove it, Mao sought to better relations

with Burma by offering to exchange animals from their national zoos. As he was later to evidence by his "Ping-Pong diplomacy," Mao believed in unorthodox approaches that took the stuffiness out of international relations and put them on a warm, human basis which people of all nations could relate to. If such ploys oversimplified the seriousness of international conflicts, they also had the merit of creating an informal, pleasant atmosphere of goodwill that encouraged solutions.

His diplomacy was not too successful with Ho Chi Minh, however. The leader of North Vietnam, struggling to free the south of his country and unite it under his Communist regime, feared Chinese hegemony almost as much as he did American intervention in support of the Saigon regime. Ho preferred Soviet aid and followed Moscow's lead in foreign policy.

Like Khrushchev, he criticized the Great Leap Forward and also expressed a wish to see a relaxation of tension between East and West. He even mocked Mao's encyclopedic pretensions. "If there's a subject Chairman Mao hasn't written about," he laughed to a reporter, "tell me and I'll try to fill the gap." But Mao was forced to match Moscow's help to Ho to try to keep American bases out of Southeast Asia and to keep North Vietnam from becoming a Soviet satellite.

Mao's contempt for Khrushchev increased when the Russian leader flew to the United States for "peaceful coexistence" talks with Eisenhower at Camp David, Maryland. The American press began waxing enthusiastic over "the spirit of Camp David." On September 30, 1959, Khrushchev flew on to Peking, hoping to cajole Mao into sharing some of that spirit.

"Imperialist war is not inevitable," he assured Mao and painted a glowing picture of Eisenhower's good faith. At a diplomatic dinner, speaking over Mao's head to the CCP Politburo, he made a speech questioning the judgment of those who sought to "test by force the stability of the capitalist system." Mao's farewell was understandably frosty. Leaving without any concessions, Khrushchev angrily snapped that Mao could forget about any resumption of Russian assistance in developing Chinese nuclear weapons.

In 1960 Mao was delighted when Khrushchev's summit meeting with the West broke up in chaos after the Russians discovered and shot down an American spy plane flying over their territory. Maybe now, Mao told Chou En-lai, Khrushchev would learn that only a fool trusted imperialist powers. He set Chou to making speeches attacking the coexistence policy.

At a Romanian Communist party congress that June, Khrushchev lashed back by attacking the Chinese as "madmen" eager to unleash nuclear war. The Chinese delegate replied by accusing Khrushchev of "revisionism." When the Congress broke up, it was clear that there was now a major and open rift between the world's two great Communist powers.

Mao moved swiftly to challenge Khrushchev for leadership of the Communist world, giving aid and advice to revolutionary movements in both hemispheres. In September, 1960, receiving Algerian rebel leader Ferhat Abbas in Peking, he encouraged him to persevere in the struggle against France.

"During our Long March we were sometimes reduced to a force of seventeen thousand," he told Abbas. "This did not prevent our victory. Hold out for real and solid independence. . . . The longer the struggle lasts, the more your enemy's position deteriorates. . . . Time is on your side."

He warned Abbas not to execute opponents or prisoners but to persuade and "reeducate" them. The former Emperor of China, he revealed, had been "reeducated" in prison and was now free in Peking, employed as a botanist.

Promising Chinese aid, Mao cautioned Abbas against turning to the United Nations for help. It had become an instrument of American foreign policy, he charged, as proved by United Nations support of the war against North Korea.

Busy with his world chess game, Mao withdrew more and more from public view. Once a year, however, on the anniversary of the founding of the Republic, hundreds of thousands of Chinese surged into the central square of Peking, eager for a glimpse of their idol on the platform beneath his ten-foot banner portrait. Despite the failure of the Great Leap Forward, Mao remained a patron saint for most Chinese. Part of this reverence had been cultivated artificially by the personality cult of Maoism, but part stemmed from the genuine gratitude of the Chinese people for Mao's deliverance of them from oppression by warlords and landlords.

At the anniversary celebration in 1960 French correspondent Bernard Ullman was close enough to write a verbal snapshot of Mao as he appeared at the age of sixty-seven:

> Mao, smoking cigarette after cigarette, his eyes half-closed, seemed far away. With a vast forehead, protruding cheekbones, a skin so smooth as to be almost shiny, his face bore an expression of total peace. . . . Clearly visible, slightly to the left of the chin, a mole, surely the world's most famous. . . . The massive body remained completely motionless and so did the expression on Mao's face. Truly, he seemed molded of different stuff from those surrounding him, impervious to human passions.

The crowd roared acclaim, shouting his name over and over again in agonized, breathless chants. Many people stood on tiptoe in the hope that somehow, magically, the Chairman would notice them personally. They sang "The East Is Red":

> China has seen the birth of a Mao Tse-tung,
> His plans bring well-being to the people,
> He is the people's great savior.

Pleased, Mao waved his gray cap in response.

Relations with Khrushchev steadily worsened. Despite Mao's efforts, he was able to woo away only one ally from Moscow—tiny Albania, led by Enver Hoxha. In Moscow, at the Twenty-second Congress of the Communist party in October, 1961, Khrushchev lashed out at the Albanians, warning them to renounce their anti-Soviet views. Chou En-lai, leading the Chinese delegation, rose to proclaim China's support for Albania.

He infuriated Khrushchev by censuring him for baring an internal Communist dispute to the capitalist West. Before leaving Moscow, Chou then went to Red Square and laid a wreath inscribed "The great Marxist-Leninist" at the foot of Joseph Stalin's embalmed body in the mausoleum—a diplomatic slap in the face for Khrushchev. The enraged Russian leader ordered Stalin's remains removed from Lenin's tomb and reburied in a simple grave under the Kremlin wall.

By the spring of 1962 the industrial economy of China was in grave trouble. Half the factories of Peking were forced to close for lack of fuel, raw materials, and spare parts. Compelled to admit that there were no jobs for twenty million Chinese in the cities and towns, the government urged them to go to the countryside and work in the communes.

Cadres loyal to Mao held meetings around the country explaining that the fault was not his but Khrushchev's. As early as 1958, they said, Mao had wanted to concentrate on agriculture and let industry wait. But, no, the Russian advisers in China had had too much influence. It was *they* who had pushed the Great Leap Forward while pretending to be against it!

Thousands of Chinese sought to escape the hungry cities by swimming or sailing sampans to Hong Kong and Macao. One refugee, asked why the Chinese did not revolt if they were dissatisfied, replied, "Because anyone who shows his discontent is arrested. Because there are only twenty-five pounds of rice each month for each worker, and even this is held back if they are not sure of your loyalty. How could we revolt?"

Yet even during the worst of the Chinese depression of 1959–1962, the Chinese people still considered themselves better off than they had been for centuries. A *Newsweek* reporter found them hungry but not in a famine condition. He also noted, "The intellectuals . . . Confucian scholars and medical technicians, have been given greater freedom —and an increased ration." It could not be denied, though, that the Great Leap had caused great suffering throughout China.

Mao grew alarmed as American U-2 spy planes began flying reconnaissance missions over China from Formosa. He became convinced of a western plot to attack his country in her time of weakness before he could develop and stockpile nuclear weapons. Hadn't the new President, John F. Kennedy, sought to overthrow Fidel Castro with an attack on Cuba's Bay of Pigs?

Mao worked out the probable strategy of China's enemies for the CCP Politburo. Chiang's troops would make a seaborne and airborne invasion in the east. United States planes would attack from Thailand and South Vietnam. The Soviet Union would grab Sinkiang Province west of Mongolia, and India would seize Tibet. It was important, Mao insisted, to throw the plotters off balance by letting them know they would not catch China by surprise and would face fierce resistance.

In Warsaw the Chinese ambassador coldly warned the puzzled American ambassador that aggression by the United States and the "Chiang Kai-shek clique" would be bloodily repulsed. A similar warning was conveyed to Khrushchev by the Chinese ambassador in Moscow. Nehru received his warning in Mao's sudden decision to press an old dispute with India over the Chinese-Indian border in the Himalayas.

When Khrushchev at once promised Nehru to furnish Soviet MIG fighters to India, Mao saw this as proof that he was right about the secret plot against China he suspected. He ordered the Red Army to attack Indian troops on the border, driving them out of thirty-five thousand square miles of the disputed territory.

Nehru was now clearly helpless to stop a full-scale Chinese invasion. To the surprise of the world the Red Army abruptly withdrew. Mao declared the border region a "demilitarized zone" and called for peaceful negotiations with Nehru.

"We will certainly not take a single inch of territory which belongs to others," a Chinese delegate told a gathering of Asian nations in Tokyo. "But on the other hand we will not permit a single inch of our territory to be taken from us by force."

The attack alienated Nehru and other neutralist leaders who had stood apart from the Cold War. Some western delegations at the United Nations, pressing their opportunity, sought to get the neutral Asian-African bloc to condemn Mao's action in India. The move failed. "After all," said an African delegate, "China is the victor, and she voluntarily withdraws her troops and offers to negotiate. What more does India want?"

A bitter Indian official replied, "Chinese policy has always been, *'Dah, dah! Tahn, tah! Dah, dah!'*—'Fight for a while; talk for a while; fight again!'"

But Mao felt satisfied with his ploy. He had demonstrated China's strength and readiness to fight in defense of its borders, as well as India's weakness. It was a hint to those

Asian leaders aligned with Nehru as to where the real power lay in Asia. They would think twice before joining any plot to invade the Chinese People's Republic.

Wooing Indonesia as an ally, Mao invited President Achmed Sukarno to Peking and paid him a rare honor. His wife, Chiang Ch'ing, made an unprecedented public appearance at a reception for the Sukarnos. Now in her early forties, her sudden emergence in the limelight at Mao's side spurred a buzz of speculation. Was she being groomed for a new political role?

Long March veterans of the Politburo recalled their suspicions of her political ambitions and her promise to stay out of the public eye if they agreed to Mao's divorce of Ho Tzu-chen in order to marry her. Why had it been broken?

Mao, in turn, was suspicious of what he saw as a right-wing trend among bureaucrats of the Politburo and the party. It seemed to him that Liu Shao-ch'i, Peking Mayor Peng Chen, and other CCP leaders were becoming revisionists promulgating Khrushchev's "phony communism," encouraging the Chinese people to relax and forget about building the revolution.

In the fall of 1962 the United States discovered that Khrushchev was secretly installing Soviet missiles in Cuba. In a dramatic confrontation that alarmed the world, Kennedy forced the Russian leader to remove them.

Delighted at Khrushchev's public humiliation, Mao used the Chinese press to brand him an inept and craven fool. *Pravda* furiously denounced Mao as "out of touch with reality . . . shut off from the world by some sort of blinders."

"We publish all the 'masterpieces' in which you rail at us," the Peking *People's Daily* taunted Khrushchev. "Do you dare do the same and publish our criticisms in Russia?"

# Chapter 14

# The Red Giants Fall Out

*"The most dangerous prospect that mankind may ever have to face is a Genghis Khan with a telephone."*

—Leo Tolstoy

The more Khrushchev sought to avoid a fatal clash with the United States, the less militant a posture he struck upon the world stage. At the same time that he urged peaceful coexistence, he could not credibly encourage revolutionary warfare.

Mao lost no opportunity to fill the vacuum he now saw in ideological leadership of the world revolutionary movement. When Robert Williams, a black-power leader in political exile from the United States, fled to China, Mao welcomed him personally over Radio Peking. Mao declared his support for American blacks in their fight for racial equality.

"I call on the workers, peasants, revolutionary intellectuals, enlightened elements of the bourgeoisie, and other enlightened persons of all colors in the world, whether white, black, yellow or brown," he appealed, "to oppose the racial discrimination practiced by U.S. imperialism. . . . We [nonwhites] are in the majority and they are in the minority . . . less than ten percent of the world's three billion people."

In 1963 Mao sent Premier Chou En-lai to Africa to encourage revolutionary movements on that continent, offering Chinese aid and guidance. Praising wars of national liberation in colonial countries, Mao called them "a mighty revolutionary storm that makes the imperialists and colonialists tremble and the revolutionary people of the world rejoice." He added, "The imperialists and colonialists say, 'An awful mess!' Revolutionary people say, 'Very good indeed!' "

In July he agreed to send a delegation to Moscow for a last-ditch effort to avert a total Sino-Soviet split. The Chinese demanded that Khrushchev join a "United Front against American imperialism." The Russians refused, charging that Mao underestimated the terrors of nuclear war and thought of war only in the archaic terms of the Long March guerrilla days. The last link between the Red giants snapped.

That same month Khrushchev signed a nuclear test ban treaty with the United States. The Chinese press instantly denounced the Russian leader as a cowardly traitor allied with imperialism who strove to restore capitalism in the Soviet Union and sabotage Marxism-Leninism throughout the world.

Mao, replied the Soviet press, was a "senile Trotskyite tyrant and racist who seeks world war, who has made monumental blunders in policy, who maintains concentration camps and massacres minority peoples, forcing them to seek refuge in the Soviet Union." It was obvious that the cleavage in the Communist world was sharp and deep and that there would be a savage struggle between China and the Soviet Union for leadership of that world.

Meanwhile China was recovering from the Great Leap Forward, and things were improving rapidly. The Maoist press now lost no opportunity to point out how far China had come in thirteen years under the Chairman's guidance, despite admitted mistakes. Before the revolution, for example, Wuhan's steel production had been eight thousand tons a year. Now that city's steel mills turned out the same production in a single day.

The engineers of Wuhan, who lived as simply as the workers in the blast furnaces and rolling mills, expressed their gratitude to Chairman Mao for the amazing progress China was now making after four thousand years of backward misery.

Over three hundred thousand new dwelling units had been constructed since the revolution. The lucky few who occupied their eighty-foot, four-room apartments paid only $2.50 a month rent out of an average monthly paycheck of $46. At housing-development nursery schools, workers' children learned Chinese characters, sang and danced, and enjoyed eggs, fish, and rice for lunch.

"When I see these happy children," one Chinese told French journalist Jules Roy, "I remember what my childhood was like. . . . When my mother found a sweet potato to give me for lunch, my hunger left me for a time and I could think of nothing I wanted more than another potato at night. You cannot imagine what China was like, the extent of its misery, just fifteen years ago. And who worked to give us a country? Chiang Kai-shek? The Americans? The West? Chairman Mao and the party!"

When Raymond Scheyven, former Belgian Minister of Economics, made a fact-finding tour of China in 1963, he reported that "most people in the West have grave misconceptions about the Chinese mainland." Most Chinese, he observed, credited Mao for living far better than they ever had before and fully supported his totalitarian government.

But the Red Chinese were also the most propagandized people on earth. Libraries and bookstores were filled with the works of Mao. Building walls everywhere bore painted slogans: "LONG LIVE CHAIRMAN MAO!" . . . "SUCCESS TO THE 5-YEAR PLAN!" . . . "CELEBRATE THE 15TH ANNIVERSARY OF THE PEOPLE'S REPUBLIC BY REDOUBLING YOUR EFFORTS IN EVERY FIELD!" Enormous posters showed soldier, peasant, and worker side by side, clutching Mao's works to their hearts to solve their problems, as they marched together toward socialist achievement.

In the villages loudspeakers blared government-slanted news bulletins interspersed with patriotic music. Party cadres urged everyone to work hard and long because they were now working for themselves and their children, not for foreign capitalists.

To protect farmland, women of all ages carted basketloads of earth and stone through rice fields to build antiflood dikes. Older women remembered being beaten as slaves by powerful landlords. Men who pulled heavy carts were cheerful, recalling hungry days when they had been forced to beg in the streets. Wharf laborers bent under cargoes still had vivid memories of foreign gunboats crashing into native junks that didn't get out of the way fast enough.

If their life was hard, did not Chairman Mao live as simply and austerely as they did? Was not everything he did for the benefit of the Chinese masses—not for warlords, rich officials, or foreign imperialists? If he urged them to clean, sweep, and polish China, was it not for their benefit? In the lake district of Hupeh the people had turned out en masse to destroy every breeding place of mosquitoes, fleas, and flies, and now their district was insect-free. Did it not pay to follow the wise way of Chairman Mao?

Mao himself, however, grew increasingly dissatisfied at what he saw as a countrywide slackening of revolutionary spirit and effort. He blamed the leadership at all levels. There was too much bureaucracy, too much privilege, too much contempt for the masses, too much selfishness.

He decided to organize a nationwide campaign in the spirit of the Long March to inspire a new revolutionary dedication and self-sacrifice in all Chinese leadership. It was signaled by the appearance in May, 1964, of a little red book that was soon to become famous, *Quotations from Chairman Mao.* Significantly, it was published by the Political Department of the Red Army. Once before the Red Army had helped him smash all obstacles to the revolution. He now relied on it to do so for him once again.

First, though, he decided that the Red Army itself must be reformed. To revive the democratic spirit of the Long March, Mao ordered all officers, including generals, to give up their rank for one month. They became ordinary soldiers, sharing the lives and work of the privates they commanded, taking orders from lowly corporals. Officers who were willing to wash their troops' socks and underwear came in for special praise.

Then Mao went to work on the intellectuals, reminding them that only the organized power of poor peasants and workers had made the revolution possible. It was therefore graceless of those who lived more comfortably not to stay in contact with the masses by soiling their hands alongside them at least once a year.

Writers, poets, playwrights, musicians, choreographers, and other intellectuals were compelled to work in rice fields to show their support for a classless society. Nuclear physicists laid bricks or worked in factories for a month to establish their Marxist credentials. Chinese officials stationed in Peking were ordered to live with the masses for one year out of every three. Not surprisingly, there was great discontent with Mao's new policy among the elite of China.

In a 1964 speech at Hanlin Academy Mao discouraged Chinese youth from "too much intellectuality." He warned them, "The reading of too many books is harmful. . . . We must read Marxist books, but we should not read too many of them either. It will be enough to read a few dozen." China's need, he emphasized, was not for more thinkers, but for more hard workers and diligent peasants.

Two almost simultaneous events in mid-October sent Mao's stock soaring in world affairs. He had urged the Kremlin Politburo, "Those who are opposed to armed uprisings must be ruthlessly kicked out as enemies, traitors and cowards." On October 14 Khrushchev was suddenly ousted for personalizing the Sino-Soviet dispute and mishandling the Cuban crisis.

Delighted, Mao congratulated Aleksei Kosygin, the new Premier, and Leonid Brezhnev, the new Soviet Communist party boss, on "the downfall of a buffoon." He was disappointed, however, when Khrushchev's successors failed to make any new conciliatory moves toward Red China. The reason may have been shock and alarm because on October 16 at 3 P.M., in remote Sinkiang Province, Mao test-exploded his first atomic bomb.

It was a dramatic punctuation mark for the October celebration of the revolution, proclaiming Red China's emergence as a world nuclear power. Tien An Men Square filled with Chinese crowds as a thousand-member band played hymns of praise to Mao and a cannon heralded his appearance on the dais. A giant parade with huge statues and pictures of Mao passed in review, and a thousand flags closed the procession.

Hundreds of thousands of Chinese roared their adulation. That night in the National Assembly three thousand singers and musicians chanted, "Beloved Chairman Mao Tse-tung, Sun that lights our heart! . . . Oh, beloved Chairman Mao, our great guide . . . our brilliant model! Following you, we will always advance courageously!"

Now that he had the power that grew out of the barrel of a nuclear reactor, Mao had to be listened to with respect in the world arena. He promptly issued a statement calling for "a world summit conference to consider nuclear disarmament." President Lyndon B. Johnson's curt reaction was to deplore Mao's nuclear program as "a tragedy for the Chinese people, who have suffered so much under the Communist regime." He did not comment on Mao's proposal that atomic weapons be outlawed and all existing nuclear stockpiles destroyed.

The western press speculated fearfully that Mao might now use China's atom bomb to launch an aggressive war of conquest. Mao scoffed at this apprehension as nonsense.

"Sooner or later," he told foreign newsmen, "these gentlemen will take a look at a map. Then they will notice that it is not China that is occupying western territory, not China that has ringed western countries with military bases, but the other way round." Wasn't China supporting revolutions? "Of course, but since when does striking blows for peace constitute warlike behavior?"

He did not disavow the reckless remarks about nuclear warfare he had made to Nehru, but he denied that he would ever initiate it. In a nuclear war, he pointed out, China would lose more people than any other nation. Any nation that went to war had a moral obligation to confine itself to the use of conventional weapons.

World leaders were not reassured, especially since Mao and Lin Piao had now worked out a new blueprint for the overthrow of world capitalism. It was inspired by their former success in isolating Chiang's forces in the cities, surrounding them from the countryside, then starving them into submission.

Once much of Asia, Africa, and Latin America ("the countryside") went Communist, Mao and Lin reasoned, the vulnerable western economies ("the cities") would collapse because they would be cut off from both raw materials and needed markets. Chinese policy, then, must concentrate on spurring agrarian revolutions everywhere. Although Mao gave them little material help, he sent advisers, propaganda materials, and some token funds. Asked for more substantial aid, he replied, "Revolution cannot be exported. Each country must make its own, as we did. You must win your own revolution with your own men and means. Otherwise it is not *your* revolution."

Mao grew alarmed in early 1965 when President Johnson began a massive bombing of North Vietnam while pouring half a million American troops into South Vietnam. This sudden escalation of that conflict revived Mao's fears of a western assault on China, which he saw as the real target of American aggression in Southeast Asia.

Preparing the Chinese people for a war of resistance against United States attack, he ordered air-raid shelters built in southern cities, stockpiled blood plasma, and evacuated the elderly, children, and nonessential workers. Some members of the CCP Politburo urged him to seek negotiations with Washington for a settlement of the Vietnam War. "The American imperialist," he replied, "will never become a Buddha and lay down his butcher knives."

Mao also saw American imperialism secretly at work in Indonesia. When he had induced Sukarno to move closer to the Red Chinese camp, a right-wing revolt overthrew Sukarno's government. Over three hundred thousand members of Indonesia's three-million-man Communist party, the PKI, were hunted down by military-led mobs and massacred in a five-month frenzy. Mao was convinced that the fine hand of the Central Intelligence Agency was behind it all; Sukarno had proof of American involvement.

In the fall of 1965 Mao's rivals in the CCP Politburo charged that his foreign policy of encouraging "perpetual revolution" in Asia, Africa, and Latin America had been a dismal failure, winning no allies for Red China. Peking could no more make over the world in its own image, they insisted, than Washington could Americanize the world.

They believed that the time had come to compromise and reach understandings with both the United States and the Soviet Union. They demanded a new program for the country that would largely ignore the outside world and concentrate on improving conditions for the Chinese people.

Mao was angered and upset by the challenge of these "bourgeois and revisionist influences" at the highest level of Chinese government. He ordered a blast in the party press against all "deviationist intellectuals," making it clear that they would have to be "restored to the thoughts of Chairman Mao."

When Ho Chi Minh visited Peking in December, Mao warned him not to listen to any revisionists in Hanoi who were urging a settlement with the United States. Ho tactfully suggested that this was a matter for the Vietnamese themselves to decide, since they were doing the fighting. But he assured Mao that Hanoi would never give up the struggle for a united and independent Vietnam.

During the winter of 1965–1966 Mao's lack of public appearances led to speculation that his health was failing. Those who caught glimpses of him reported that he moved slowly and feebly, supported by an attendant. The rumors increased when, in an interview with his old friend American journalist Edgar Snow, Mao smilingly observed that he was "getting ready to see God very soon."

Death was often on his mind these days, not apprehensively but in a philosophic vein. He was struck by the fact that although one wife and two sons, his younger sister, and his two younger brothers had all met violent deaths while serving the Chinese Communist movement, he had survived. He had often been prepared for death, but "death just did not seem to want" him. Because, perhaps, destiny still needed him at the helm of China to protect and preserve the revolution?

It worried Mao that the purity of the revolution might

not survive his death. "Who knows what will happen in a few decades?" he gloomily asked André Malraux in 1965. "Intellectuals are against Marxism. Neither our agricultural nor our industrial problems have been solved. The problems of youth, even less so."

To "purify Marxist thought" in China, Mao sought to purge the ranks of China's leading writers and teachers. The purge spread to the Chinese press and the whole Communist party apparatus. Pamphlets denouncing "revisionists" flooded through the country in a mounting paper tidal wave.

Chief target of Mao's attack was President Liu Shao-ch'i, who was accused of masterminding the movement to force Peking to come to terms with Moscow. Liu replied that a more flexible foreign policy would have far more advantages for China. An alliance with the Soviet Union would mean coordinated Sino-Soviet anti-American aid to North Vietnam. It would also win back for China badly needed Russian technicians and trade.

Mao's opponents pointed to Cuba as the latest example of the failure of his foreign policy. Mao had relied heavily on Cuba as a staging area for revolutionary aid to Latin America. But in March, 1966, Castro, who had moved closer to the Soviet Union, made it clear that his hospitality to the Chinese was wearing thin. He attacked Mao as senile and barbarous, accused the Red Chinese of "launching an imperialist-type campaign against Cuba," and threatened to break off diplomatic relations. Was it "revisionism" to suggest that a strategy that had lost Fidel Castro seriously needed changing?

Mao stood his ground firmly. Convinced that war with the United States was imminent, he sought to inspire his people with a new revolutionary zeal that would make them capable of withstanding a major nuclear attack. "Bourgeois elements" who could not be relied upon would have to be ousted from power, however high the positions they occupied.

He began by further democratizing the Red Army, abolishing all military ranks, and returning to the old revolutionary tradition when all ranks were simply "comrades." Party bureaucrats were warned they would no longer be permitted to remain an elite cut off from contact with the people. Red China would stay Red. It would not be allowed to "degenerate" into Moscow's brand of "bourgeois decayed socialism."

"The party organization of any locality that goes against Comrade Mao Tse-tung must be opposed," shrilled the *People's Daily.* "We shall crush those persons in authority who have taken the road leading toward the restoration of capitalism!"

The purge was on.

# Chapter 15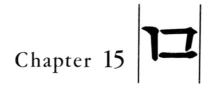

# The Cultural Revolution

The affairs of the party and government had gradually passed into the hands of pragmatic administrators and technicians who paid dutiful lip service to the powers of Maoist thought while systematically ignoring his precepts. It was Liu Shao-ch'i and his supporters in the CCP Central Committee who ran the superstructure, the labor unions, the party schools, and cadre organizations in Mao's name.

They believed that the revolution should now be allowed to recede into Chinese history as no longer relevant, like the American Revolution in the United States and the Bolshevik Revolution in the Soviet Union. What was the point of a revolution if those who had led it couldn't finally relax and enjoy its blessings in peace and prosperity?

To Mao this was rank heresy. The revolution was his pyramid, the glorious accomplishment to which he had devoted his life. He was determined that his brand of communism should not degenerate after his death into bourgeois Sovietism. The Chinese people must be kept in a permanent state of revolutionary ferment to keep their society dynamic.

Seeking to smash the bureaucracy that thwarted his will, Mao turned to the two people closest to him he trusted most —his wife, Chiang Ch'ing, and fifty-nine-year-old Lin Piao, the old Long March comrade whose personal loyalty had never wavered. In the summer of 1966 Mao made his wife a member of the CCP Central Committee. By November she was Lin's deputy in charge of organizing a new "cultural revolution." Her first task was to "reform" Chinese music, opera, and art by bringing practitioners of those arts in line with Maoist thought. Chiang Ch'ing spoke over Radio Peking denouncing rock music, jazz, impressionism, and abstract art as western lures "intended to poison and paralyze the minds of the people."

It was to the youth of China that Mao chiefly looked to carry the revolutionary torch when it fell from his hands, but the young, he fretted, were too soft. Chinese youth had never known the hardships of life under imperialism, fought a war, or experienced the exhilaration of making desperate sacrifices for the revolution. Reading about history or hearing about it from parents was a poor substitute for the real thing. They might easily be corrupted into making peace with imperialists or even letting Chiang Kai-shek return. "Whether or not we can successfully prevent the emergence of Khrushchev's revisionism in China," he warned, "is a matter of life and death for our party and our country."

In February, 1966, Mao ordered hundreds of thousands of high-school and college students shipped to village communes to work beside the peasants. Putting calluses on their hands and spirits, they would learn the hard lessons of past struggle. Party cadres would instill in them discipline, loyalty to the masses, self-sacrifice, and revolutionary zeal.

They would play a major role themselves in a new revolutionary movement, instead of simply listening to the tales of their grandfathers' heroic deeds on the Long March or their fathers' struggles against the Japanese and Chiang. Then Mao would be able to depend upon them not to liquidate the revolution he and his comrades had sacrificed so much to win.

A new drive indoctrinated all Chinese children, from the age of seven, to believe that they could find the answers to all problems, personal and civic, in the Thoughts of Chairman Mao. One commune in South Shansi reported what had happened when cottonfields had been invaded by insects that were destroying the crop. An essay by Mao, read aloud at a mass meeting, had inspired 250 young volunteers to sleep in the mountainside fields for a week. Crawling on all fours, they had destroyed seventy thousand insects and saved the harvest.

In the spring of 1966 Mao and Lin fired the opening guns of their party purge. In Peking a wall poster was pasted up announcing that Mayor Peng Chen and the whole City Council had been replaced by a People's Commune. Unaware of what had happened, Peng sought to enter his office that day, but his way was barred by the Red Army. Lin Piao then seized control of Peking's radio station and newspapers.

Universities throughout China were shut down while their faculties and curricula were tested for Maoist purity. Many leading Chinese intellectuals rushed to save their skins by seeking to absolve their sins through confession. "Strictly speaking," humbly admitted Kuo Mo-jo, seventy-four-year-old president of the Chinese Academy of Science, "according to the standards of today, all that I have written should be burned."

Mao now organized some six million high-school and college students into a new militant force called the Red Guard, with the youngest members later channeled into the Young Pioneers. Lin Piao defined their objective—"the protection of Chairman Mao and his teachings from Chinese reactionaries." When the Red Guard's activities became increasingly confused and violent, there was speculation that Mao and Lin had lost control of them.

Their emergence indicated a break with, or bypass of,

established cadres of the regular party organization. Alarmed, Liu Shao-ch'i met the challenge by calling for an emergency session of the CCP Central Committee to demand that Mao either call off the Red Guard or resign as party Chairman. Having counted noses, Liu was confident that his faction had a comfortable majority of the 165 Central Committee votes.

Meanwhile rumors thickened that Mao had had a stroke and was failing fast. He had not been seen in public for over half a year. Radio Peking branded the rumors "nonsense . . . malicious, false rumors of imperialism."

In July, 1966, Mao suddenly took a highly publicized nine-mile swim in the Yangtze near Wuhan, his favorite vacation retreat. Dozens of photographers were on hand to record this proof of his physical, moral, and intellectual vitality. "Chairman Mao's swim invigorated everyone's heart," enthused Radio Peking, "and brought immense inspiration to everybody."

The London *Daily Mirror,* running one picture, suggested irreverently that during the "Great Splash Forward" Mao had been held afloat from beneath "by inscrutable Chinese frogmen." There was little doubt, though, that seventy-three-year-old Mao was still in reasonably good shape as he waved exuberantly to crowds watching the "swim-in," which included five thousand swimmers towing floats with signs like: "THE IMPERIALISTS ARE PUSHING CHINA AROUND IN A WAY THAT CHINA MUST DEAL WITH THEM SEVERELY!"

Mao managed to postpone the emergency session of the CCP Central Committee demanded by Liu Shao-ch'i until his supporters had time to win over some doubtful votes. Then in a stormy meeting Mao's faction narrowly outvoted Liu's.

Although Liu was permitted to remain temporarily as President of the Republic, he was stripped of party powers.

Defense Minister Lin Piao moved up in the hierarchy to replace him, second in power now to only Mao himself.

As part of the cultural revolution, Lin was flooding the country with copies of *Quotations from Chairman Mao.* Chiang Ch'ing made it the Bible of the Red Guard and ordered the youngsters to chant Mao's thoughts in unison to indoctrinate people. What went on in Chairman Mao's mind, she explained, held "all the truths that ever had been or would be."

The full-scale campaign of the Great Proletarian Cultural Revolution (GPCR) was opened officially on August 18, 1966, by a mass rally of Red Guards and Young Pioneers jammed solidly into the Gate of Heavenly Peace Square. The opening of China's schools and colleges had been postponed for four months. During this holiday an estimated fourteen million youths would fan out to every corner of the country, their mission to purge all officials, bureaucrats, and cadres known to oppose the Thoughts of Chairman Mao.

Over a million youngsters aged thirteen to twenty-four gathered in Peking's great square at dawn, singing "The East Is Red." Flowers in the hands of one hundred thousand formed the characters "LONG LIVE CHAIRMAN MAO." Worshipful hysteria greeted the first glimpse of Mao, who wore a plain grass-green military tunic and cap with Red star to emphasize the military nature of the crusade.

Mao promised the youth to turn China into a "great school" where peasants would study politics, soldiers would learn how to run factories, and bureaucrats would acquire farming skills. They roared with delight when he encouraged them to spread out through China and "declare war on the old world."

Hordes of Red Guards were soon surging through dozens of cities spreading terror in a manner reminiscent of the old Boxer Rebellion. They invaded homes—even the home of Madame Sun Yat-sen—and humiliated inhabitants verbally and physically, parading some officials through the streets in dunce caps. They attacked temples and churches; invaded museums to destroy western modern art; sacked shops and ripped western-style clothes.

Tens of thousands of people were savagely beaten with sticks, and several thousand died. Police were forbidden to interfere. The power-drunk students, hair cut short, sang revolutionary songs as they surged through China purging it of "reactionary elements." They chanted, "Everything that does not reflect the Thought of Mao Tse-tung must burn!"

Frightened foreigners declared that it seemed as though Mao had declared war on China itself, or at least on all who retained ties with China's past or the West. Victims included old people who buried their dead instead of cremating them and burned incense and joss sticks to honor them, and bookshop-owners whose windows were not filled with Mao's works.

The Red Guard was soon in total command of the streets of all Chinese cities, deriding or attacking everything old or foreign, intimidating local authorities. Old street signs were torn down and replaced by revolutionary names. External Peace Boulevard became The East Is Red Boulevard; Well of the Prince's Palace was renamed Prevent Revision Street.

Although all Red Guards were volunteers, and eager ones, Mao's GPCR forces mobilized them from all over China, transported them hundreds of miles, fed them, lodged them, and rallied them at Peking and other large cities. They were encouraged to carry on their assaults on local dignitaries and ancient traditions in roving bands of twenty to fifty youths, without fear of reprisal or arrest. In Shanghai they beat up the deputy mayor and in Canton attacked a group of glass-factory workers who did not display enough revolutionary zeal.

Mao laid the groundwork for a drive against China's "overeducated intellectuals" by questioning their claims to prestige. "It is reported that penicillin was invented by a laundryman in a dyer's shop," he alleged. "Benjamin Franklin of America discovered electricity, although he began as a newspaper boy. Confucius got started at twenty-three. What learning did Jesus have? Sakyamuni created Buddhism when he was nineteen. When Marx first created dialectical materialism, he was very young. He acquired his learning later . . . It is always those with less learning who overthrow those with more learning."

Mao was now skeptical of the usefulness of higher education. Had not his own most profound learning experiences come from self-study and from living among the peasantry? Why, then, should this not be the way for 375 million Chinese under the age of twenty? The Great Proletarian Cultural Revolution would enable youth to "learn revolution-making by making revolution." The Red Guard were clearly getting Mao's message. At the University of Peking, China's most respected seat of learning, elderly professors were forced to run a gauntlet between Red Guard ranks while they were spat upon.

The Maoist press kept up a running attack on the old-line CCP apparatus, denouncing high party members and functionaries as "counterrevolutionary intellectuals" and "poisonous weeds" that had to be uprooted. In Peking Mayor Peng Chen was accused of having bugged Mao's headquarters and passing on secret information to the Russians. All over China Red Guards clashed with local cadres at party headquarters.

Chiang Ch'ing urged Mao to make a clean sweep of his enemies by executing them, beginning with Liu Shao-ch'i; but that was too much for her husband, who believed in reforming his foes rather than killing them. He prudently remembered, moreover, the worldwide condemnation that had fallen on Stalin in the thirties for bloodily liquidating his political enemies in the Russian purge.

In broadcasts beamed at Red China, Moscow charged that Mao's GPCR had taken a death toll of ten million people, or more than all Chinese casualties during the war with Japan; and that millions more had been sent to labor camps and jails to be tormented or tortured into "confessing" mistakes.

Mao, insisted Moscow, had clearly gone mad in his determination to smash traditional Chinese respect for age and authority that he considered a conservative anchor dragging at revolutionary progress. The Kremlin view was scarcely objective, especially since Soviet and Chinese troops were now skirmishing along the Sino-Soviet border.

An American correspondent in Hong Kong called the GPCR "a tremendous McCarthyite witch-hunt, Red style." A Japanese correspondent in Peking reported, "It's complete chaos."

Mao saw China's convulsions as therapeutic, however. The struggle would purify it of poisons in the body politic. Civil war did not alarm him; he had risen to power through civil war. He intended his Cultural Revolution to last fifty to one hundred years, if necessary, to erase the last "imperialists, revisionists and reactionaries" from the land and instill a permanent revolutionary consciousness in his people.

In a deeper sense the GPCR represented Mao's power struggle with death—not personal death, but death of the revolution he had dominated for so long. If he could leave it behind intact and imperishable, personal death would mean nothing because he would be assured of immortality through his revolution without end.

He was driven by the same instinct that drives an author to seek to preserve his works for as long as possible after he has personally vanished from the scene. Religious people aspired to an afterlife in heaven; atheist Mao conceived of an afterlife only as the survival of his influence on earth.

Gnawed by secret anxiety that Maoism might have become obsolete, no longer relevant to China's modern problems, he insisted that Chinese of the future must continue to be guided by his writings, thoughts, and guerrilla experiences of two and three decades earlier. In a word, he angrily resisted being shelved or ignored as an old fogy living dreamily in the past, out of touch with the present and future.

Mao's political enemies wanted stability, not ferment, for China. Mao's way, they were convinced, meant only chaos, disrupted production and shortages, and the constant threat of war. But to Mao stability and calm in national affairs meant revolutionary stagnation and the growth of conservatism. The Russians, he warned, had made this mistake, and now the Russian people would never achieve the true communism they had been promised by Marx and Lenin.

By February, 1967, the Roman holiday of the Red Guards was over, and it appeared that Mao had won the political struggle against his rivals. His supporters gradually emerged in control of key municipal and provincial organizations. The old CCP leaders had either been removed from office, "reformed," or had their powers clipped. When most Red Guards went back to school, their control of China was taken over by the Red Army, under whom they had functioned as "reserves."

Mao had clearly broken the subordination of the military to the party elite. Although seventy-three ranking generals of doubtful personal loyalty to Mao had also had to be purged, the purified Red Army under Lin Piao had been raised to a paramount position. The end result was to entrench Maoism firmly as China's path to the future.

Mao had a fresh shock in store for the world in June, only

twenty-six months after China had achieved nuclear fission. Without help from the Soviet Union the Chinese successfully tested a hydrogen bomb. The world's nuclear and military experts were dumbfounded. It had taken the United States over seven years to bridge that gap, and France hadn't yet managed it even after eight years. How had the Chinese done it? "Chairman Mao's thought!" beamed Radio Peking.

Secretary of State Dean Rusk now appealed for world support of the American attempt, through the unpopular Vietnam War, to contain "a billion Chinese armed with nuclear weapons." His plea met with little credibility, especially since Washington continued to turn a deaf ear to Mao's call for an international agreement to destroy all nuclear weapons.

Thousands of Red Guards who decided not to return to school continued to demonstrate and riot in the cities. Their targets now were principally foreigners. One mob burned the British chancery in Peking to the ground. But no foreigners received rougher treatment than the Russians. Chinese rioters attacked Soviet diplomats, damaged their cars, and demonstrated violently against the Russian Embassy.

"Filth, swine, hyenas, rascals, scoundrels!" they shrieked. The Kremlin reacted furiously. "Never before in all the history of the Soviet state," fumed *Tass,* "has such an unbridled anti-Soviet campaign been conducted in any country, even those most hostile to the Soviet Union."

Moscow arranged an emergency airlift of over two hundred embassy wives and children from Peking. They were forced to run a gauntlet of howling Chinese mobs to escape onto Soviet planes. It was obvious from the lack of any attempt to restrain the rioters that they had Mao's approval.

The Kremlin did not break off diplomatic relations, nevertheless, perhaps counting on the death of Chairman Mao to bring a less fanatical Chinese leader to power. But half a dozen other countries whose diplomats had been molested either severed or suspended diplomatic relations with Peking.

Mao was unimpressed. The fewer outside influences in China, the better. The Maoist press, under Chiang Ch'ing's guidance, derided the giants of western culture—Shakespeare, Beethoven, Molière, Tolstoy—as "revisionist squids."

Hardly anything was read now in China but the works of Chairman Mao. To be without one's little red book was suspect. It was quoted aloud in the street, on buses, trains, and planes. By January, 1968, over 350 million copies had been distributed, making the Gideon promotion of the Bible a modest effort in comparison.

The Chinese people, young and old, were persistently reminded that if they studied the Thought of Mao Tse-tung, they would be able to shoot a rifle straighter, solve all problems quicker, hit a Ping-Pong ball harder, and produce more grain and steel. The Peking press cited constant examples.

A locomotive driver credited Maoist thought for being able to increase his speed, despite driving "a rotten old piece of goods sold us by the Soviet Union." Peking doctors reported that patients studying the little red book recovered from burn trauma 95 percent more often than those who didn't; and others who read it during surgery without anesthesia had felt no pain. Champions of Ping-Pong tournaments credited Chairman Mao's Thoughts for their triumphs. This last item caught Mao's eye and gave him an idea that would soon astonish the world once more.

# Chapter 16

# Ping-Pong Diplomacy

In the October, 1967, issue of *Foreign Affairs* American Presidential aspirant Richard M. Nixon took Mao to task for his obduracy in refusing to follow the Russian example and seek a peaceful accommodation with the West:

> The world cannot be safe until China changes. Thus our aim . . . should be to induce change. The way to do this is to persuade China that it *must* change; that it cannot satisfy its imperial ambitions, and that its own national interest requires a turning away from foreign adventuring and a turning inward toward the solution of its own domestic problems.

Nixon declared that America's long-range aim should be to "pull China back into the family of nations" by persuading Mao that the great powers were not "ganging up" on China and had no racist feelings against her. But as a short-range policy he advocated forging a strong alliance of Asian nations to contain China, backed by American power—"a marshalling of Asian forces both to keep the peace and to help draw off the poison from the thoughts of Mao." He concluded:

> Dealing with Red China is something like trying to cope with the more explosive ghetto elements in our country. In each case a potentially destructive force has to be curbed . . . an outlaw element

has to be brought within the law . . . dialogues have to be opened
. . . aggression has to be restrained while education proceeds.
. . . In neither case can we afford to let those now self-exiled from
society stay exiled forever.

When Richard Nixon was elected President little over a year later, Mao knew exactly what Asian policies he could expect from the new Republican administration.

Meanwhile Johnson's Secretary of State, Dean Rusk, kept insisting that if China gave up her aggressive policies, the United States would be willing to withdraw from Vietnam. Mao replied curtly that he had no aggressive policies to abandon. China had sent aid to Hanoi and other revolutionary regimes, yes—just as Washington was supporting counterrevolutionary regimes all over the world—but it was not China who had sent troops and bombers to Vietnam. Who, then, Mao demanded, was guilty of aggression?

He noted with satisfaction that all over the world his revolutionary thoughts were beginning to take root in the ideas of many young and left-wing intellectuals. They were impressed with Mao's conviction that the principal concern of men should be with the quality of human life, rather than with an accumulation of things, of materialistic comfort. His slogan for Chinese youth, "To rebel is justified," and his attacks on bureaucracy and the establishment were finding enthusiastic echoes among students in Europe and America.

In late 1967 a French Maoist hurled a plastic bomb into a prison courtyard to protest the arrest of a farmer during agricultural strikes. In Berlin demonstrating university students led by German Maoists forced the resignation of Socialist Mayor Heinrich Albertz. "At a time when Communist China has scarcely a friend to call its own on this earth," observed German academician Klaus Mehnert, "Mao has suddenly become the ideological leader of a part of the radical youth on all continents."

Mehnert's own class included Maoists from Brazil, Kenya, Nepal, and the United States. Mao's little red book was a runaway best seller in European bookstores. Students everywhere began wearing sweaters emblazoned with Mao's face and name. The son of West German Chancellor Willy Brandt declared that he and his friends sympathized with Maoism because "we want to eliminate the domination of one man by another."

Rudi "Red" Dutschke, student leader at Berlin's Free University, led violent demonstrations against police. "We must sweep aside the bureaucracy," he insisted, "that layer of civil servants, parties and governments, just as Mao is using the Red Guards to destroy the bureaucracy of China."

At the very same time, ironically, many Chinese youths were becoming disillusioned with Mao for "turning off" their revolution. Having enjoyed the excitement of revolt, many were unwilling to settle down to the humdrum tasks of study. Others, after the exhilarating rallies and demonstrations in the cities, found life on the commune too dull.

Some young people began to hold underground meetings to question the Thought of Chairman Mao. Embarrassing questions were raised. If so many party cadres had to be overthrown by the GPCR, what did that say about the judgment of the Maoists who had put them there in the first place?

If Maoist foreign policy was so wise, why had it met with rebuffs in Cuba, Indonesia, Algeria, Ghana, and the Congo? Had the Red Guards, perhaps, been used by Mao simply to divert attention from his embarrassing defeats abroad?

By the beginning of 1968 Mao had quarreled with over thirty-two countries which at one time or another had sought better relations with Peking. His attempt to capture control of anticolonial movements had failed in Africa, Latin America, Indonesia, and, most notably, Vietnam, where Ho Chi Minh insisted upon remaining carefully neutral between Peking and Moscow. For all his efforts to challenge the Soviet Union as leader of the Communist world, Mao still had only tiny Albania in his camp.

If he had broken the power of the party elite in China, he had done so only at the cost of letting his country slip into anarchy. The Chinese economy was heeling badly, like a storm-tossed ship with no one at the wheel. Administrators at all levels, old and new, were fearful of making decisions for which they might be criticized or attacked.

Work discipline seemed to have vanished all over China. "No more slavery" was a popular slogan, meaning the right of workers to do as they pleased and work only when they felt like it. Many organized "8–2–6" groups—going to work at eight o'clock, taking two hours for lunch, returning home at six o'clock.

Slowdowns, absenteeism, and strikes were widespread in all major industries. In the countryside purged party leaders were seeking revenge on their successors, and old feuds were flaming. In hospitals doctors subtly sabotaged medical care, in resentment at being forced to sweep up and to serve patients meals as well as operate on them. To show how Maoist they had become, they told patients with complaints, "Well, just read Volume II of Chairman Mao's works, and you'll feel better right away."

"We have won a great victory," Mao insisted in October, 1968, "but the defeated class will still struggle. These people are still around, and this class still exists. Therefore we cannot speak of *final* victory. Not for decades."

Border clashes along the 3,500-mile Sino-Soviet frontier, meanwhile, were growing more serious. Soviet party boss Leonid Brezhnev warned that the situation was "reaching a point where everything is possible." By the spring of 1969 there was heavy fighting over a disputed island in a border river, and the Russians began war maneuvers in eastern Siberia. In May, however, Mao suddenly told

Brezhnev that he was willing to negotiate their border differences—another example of the "fight and talk" strategy he had used on Nehru.

If the Russians were never quite sure what to expect next from Mao, neither were the Americans. When Nixon's invasion of Cambodia in May, 1970, provoked antiwar demonstrations that ended in the killing of students, Mao lashed out savagely at the American President:

"While massacring the people in other countries, U.S. imperialism is slaughtering the white and black people in its own country. . . . Nixon's fascist atrocities have kindled the raging flames of the revolutionary mass movement in the United States. The Chinese people firmly support the revolutionary struggle of the American people. . . . People of the world, unite and defeat the U.S. aggressors and all their running dogs!"

Unexpectedly, however, Mao began making conciliatory gestures. The worse Sino-Soviet relations grew, the more he worried about his old nightmare—a joint U.S.–U.S.S.R. attack on Red China. He had not been able to frighten his enemies by saber-rattling. Perhaps the best way to keep them from uniting against him was to thaw his relations with Washington.

Nixon had suggested through contacts in Romania and Yugoslavia that the United States was seriously interested in developing better relations with Red China. Maybe, Mao mused, the time had come for less *dah, dah* and more *tahn, tah*. Chou En-lai had been pressing him to try a more amiable foreign policy. Now he agreed to mend China's fences abroad.

Calling for peaceful coexistence between all nations, Mao returned twenty-seven Chinese ambassadors to posts abroad from which they had been withdrawn. He personally welcomed scores of foreign delegations in return, including those of Yugoslavia and East Germany. For the first time in years hundreds of foreigners were admitted to China's cities and countryside.

Canada quickly recognized Red China, followed by Italy, France, and other countries eager to negotiate trade pacts with Mao. They found the Chinese difficult to bargain with but always prompt in paying their bills. Trade with Japan shot up in one year by 25 percent, despite some doubts by Mao about "the wild ambition of Japanese militarism to redominate Asia."

Mao's new cordiality made Red Chinese admission into the United Nations now almost a certainty. Even the United States ended its opposition, hopeful that Mao would consent to join without requiring Chiang Kai-shek to be kicked out first.

The State Department's China experts suspected that Mao's friendlier attitude toward the United States was an attempt to drive a wedge between Moscow and Washington. Mao had once quoted an old Chinese proverb, "Use barbarians to control barbarians." But closer United States–Chinese ties also suited American policy at this time by worrying the Soviet Union. Moscow might be more willing now to make concessions in United States–Soviet negotiations on arms reduction—the SALT talks.

Something was definitely in the wind when Premier Chou En-lai, still Mao's most skillful diplomat and "man for all seasons," dispatched Red China's table-tennis team to Japan for world championship matches, instructing them, "Put friendship first and competition second." That was an unusual reversal of Mao's aggressive policy of insisting upon Chinese supremacy in all things. China's Ping-Pong champions were being told to win, if they must, by only the closest of scores, in order to avoid humiliating the Japanese and other nations' contestants.

Mao's next step astonished the world. On April 19, 1971, when the competition in Tokyo ended, the Chinese team extended an invitation to the American team competing there to make a nine-day tour of China, along with three American newsmen stationed in Tokyo. It was the first formal invitation to an American group to enter China since Mao had founded the People's Republic twenty-one years earlier.

The American "Ping-Pong diplomats" won a quick okay from Washington and a week later were greeted in the Great Hall of the People in Peking by Chou himself. "You have opened a new page in the relations of the Chinese and American people," he told them affably. "I am confident that this beginning again of our friendship will certainly meet with the majority support of our two peoples. Don't you agree with me?"

The American athletes burst into enthusiastic applause. During their trip through China they were cheered warmly every step of the way, indicating popular Chinese support for Mao's decision to try Ping-Pong diplomacy. They lost against China's crack teams but only by the narrowest of margins. The Americans recognized that they were being allowed to "save face" as a hospitable gesture.

Nixon quickly responded by announcing new measures to warm up Sino-American relations. There would be a relaxation of the twenty-one-year-old embargo on United States trade with China, beginning with "nonstrategic" goods; Americans would now be permitted to visit Red China; American oil companies could sell fuel to ships or planes bound for or from China; and United States ships and planes could now carry Chinese cargoes between non-Chinese ports.

Speaking for the Democrats, Senator Mike Mansfield called these concessions "commendable" and "long overdue." Delighted with press praise for his new China policy, the President expressed cautious optimism. "What we have done is broken the ice," he explained. "Now we have to test the water to see how deep it is."

Mao indicated the depth of that water by making a new proposal through Chou En-lai. Red China was willing to help extricate the United States from its disastrous embroilment in the Vietnam War by participating with Washington in an Asian conference to bring about peace throughout Indo-China.

In a bombshell announcement on July 15, 1971, President Nixon went on television to tell the American people that his foreign policy adviser, Henry Kissinger, had made a secret visit to Peking to see Chou. Chou had invited the President to visit China to discuss such a peace conference. Presumably resumption of Sino-American diplomatic relations and Red China's admission to the United Nations would also be on the agenda.

Nixon announced that he was accepting the invitation, which amounted to *de facto* recognition of Mao's government, and would make a "journey for peace" to Peking before May, 1972. Speaking for the United Nations, Secretary-General U Thant declared, "This opens a new chapter in the history of international relations."

It was ironic that Mao, the revolutionary firebrand, should score his greatest diplomatic triumph by abandoning truculence for a good-neighbor policy. It was no less ironic that Richard Nixon, the hard-line anti-Communist conservative, should score his best points in foreign policy by extending a hand of friendship to Mao Tse-tung.

Power for Mao, unquestionably, would still continue to grow out of the barrel of a gun. In the end, however, perhaps it would be a non-Marxist idea whose time had come—Ping-Pong diplomacy—that had finally opened the door to the restoration of Red China to the community of nations.

Chapter 17

# The Thoughts of Chairman Mao

Mao Tse-tung's role in shaping modern China is best understood by the fact that he was a Chinese patriot first and a Communist second. A profound scholar of Chinese history, he felt pride in his country's early greatness and shame for its later subjection by the imperialist West. Studying the thoughts of Chinese philosophers and military strategists who had lived before him, Mao tested, revised, changed, and carried out many of their ideas, modified by his borrowings from the western cult of communism. "Mao's stroke of genius," Liu Shao-ch'i once said, "was to transpose the European character of Marxism-Leninism into its Asian form."

Coming to power through his own efforts, Mao relied heavily on his own judgment in the face of almost impossible odds, often against the advice and pressure of the Russians. He came to see a deadly parallel between the Soviet Union under communism and the Russia of the czars. Moscow, he learned, was a nationalist power far less concerned with world communism than with the preservation of its own borders and hegemony.

To both Russians and Americans Mao often seemed as inscrutable and paradoxical as his policies. Usually mild-mannered and soft-spoken, he was also quick to laugh or rage. He wrote sensitive poetry yet ordered or condoned attacks on millions of people who balked at his policies. Seemingly austere and isolated, he nevertheless had a gift for lifelong friendships and inspired adoration by the masses.

Since Chinese tradition frowned on immodest speech, dress, and behavior, Mao hid an immense self-esteem behind a surface humility. Dressing like a poor soldier, he forbade the naming of provinces, cities, or towns after himself, banned celebrations of his birthday, and accepted a monthly salary of only eighty dollars. Yet he exercised his powers as sweepingly as any Manchu emperor and encouraged the development of a Maoist idolatry that raised him to a sacred plane on a level with Buddha and Confucius.

Through most of his life Mao nourished a vision of his country's emergence out of its backwardness through the transformation of the peasantry under Communist development. He had compassion for the hardships and sufferings of the peasants and great faith in their future capacity for achievement once they were liberated from a feudal society.

For the land itself he had a mystical love strongly hinted at in his poems. In *Yellow Crane Tower* he wrote:

> Broad, broad
> through the country flow the nine tributaries.
> Deep, deep
> from north to south cuts a line.
> Blurred in the blue haze of the rain and mist
> The Snake and Tortoise Hills tower above the water. . . .
> In wine I drink a pledge to the surging torrent.
> The tide of my heart rises as high as the waves.

Something of a mystic, Mao took for his god an amorphous mass called the People. "When we say, 'We are the

Sons of the People,' " he told Malraux, "China understands it as she understood the phrase 'Son of Heaven.' The People have taken the place of the ancestors. The People, not the victorious Communist party."

He sought to demolish the old Chinese ideology, culture, customs, and habits, which he saw as chains used by "the exploiting classes" to enslave his people for thousands of years. Commenting on Mao's ambitious attempt to make over the Chinese people, Peking's *People's Daily* observed, "This great task of transforming customs and habits is without any precedent in human history."

Maurice Ciantar, French correspondent, saw Mao as a kind of Oriental Don Quixote: "Mao Tse-tung wants to make 700 million Chinese into 700 million saints. It's a noble idea, and stupid." Former French Premier Edgar Faure described Mao as having "the gestures of a man of religion—he makes me think of the leader of a religious community."

Mao never ceased to place his faith in Chinese manpower as his country's greatest strength. Informed that seventeen hundred new Chinese were born every single hour of every single day, he beamed, "Seven hundred million people in a statistic is a good thing." Ignoring the growing problems of a world population explosion, he was confident that the Chinese people would survive every ordeal because they were so numerous that no natural or man-made disaster could destroy them.

Increasingly impressed with his own inspirations as a fountainhead of all wisdom, Mao encouraged the study of his thoughts as the best way to modernize and strengthen China. All things were possible, he believed, by the exercise of sheer willpower. A nation poor in machinery could build a large-scale industry, even atomic weaponry, simply by calling upon its enormous resources of manpower.

Steeped in the lore of old China, Mao loved to draw on

folk tales, proverbs, and quotations from classics to make his points. He was fond of relating the ancient Chinese fable of "The Foolish Old Man Who Removed the Mountains." Its hero was an old peasant who sought to move two mountains, stone by stone. Derided, he explained, "When I die, my sons will carry on. When they die, there will be my grandsons, and then their sons and grandsons, and so on to infinity." But God had taken pity on him and finished the job for him.

Modern Chinese, Mao added, knew that there was no god except the people themselves. So it was they who would move China's mountainous problems, stone by stone, without waiting for future generations to finish the job.

Like a wandering monk, Mao often turned up at this commune or that factory to talk earnestly with peasants and workers about their everyday problems. No party cadres were too remote to escape his attention, no enterprises too obscure for his inspection.

Under his goading, inspiration, and iron rule, millions of Chinese literally worked themselves to death. Old men and children broke stones in the quarries, and women carried them away, Sundays as well as weekdays. If it was a form of slavery, it was a slavery most Chinese people consented to in order to keep their country independent and to ensure a better life for their children if not for themselves. No one grew rich under Mao, but no one was forced to beg in order to survive as millions had been compelled to do before he had founded the People's Republic of China.

China and India had both been at the same level of development when Mao began his revolution. But today, in steel production alone, China's output is three times higher than India's. His industrial revolution has also made China the second strongest industrial power in Asia after Japan. Few would deny that it was Mao who transformed China from a feeble, helpless giant into one of the world's great powers.

Unlike Stalin, who ruled through his party bureaucracy and secret police, Mao distrusted the bureaucracy and drew his power from the Chinese masses. When bureaucrats balked at his plans, he bypassed them to seek "conscious action by hundreds of millions of people." The Red Army and its juvenile corps, the Red Guards, set the masses in motion, stirring China in the direction he wanted it to go.

Mao preferred to think of himself as a man of action, a thinking revolutionist, rather than as an intellectual. He grew increasingly contemptuous of bookish Communists who knew only theory and had never dirtied their hands in soil, axle grease, or enemy blood. "The more one reads, the more foolish one becomes," he grew fond of saying scornfully. "Being an unpolished man, I am not too cultivated."

No sentimentalist, he was prepared to spill as much blood as necessary to win and secure his revolution. His rule was far from benign, and there is little doubt that his was the responsibility for the millions of non-Communists who were murdered during the land-reform program and the thousands who died during the Great Proletarian Cultural Revolution. Yet the western powers who condemned him for these excesses never once rebuked Chiang Kai-shek for having massacred four fifths of the Communist membership, including women and children, without warning in Shanghai in 1927 and for the widespread atrocities committed by his armies during the next twenty years of his reign.

No gentle soul, Mao nevertheless frequently cautioned soldiers, peasants, and workers not to put to death "reactionary arch-criminals" without "fair trials" and warned, "The less killing the better." Basically, he believed in adding to his strength by converting enemies rather than killing them.

Like Stalin and Khrushchev, he ruthlessly purged the Communist party to rid himself of political rivals and opponents, yet unlike Stalin, he rarely had them shot. He felt strong bonds of loyalty toward the comrades who had accompanied him on the most meaningful event of his life, the fantastic Long March. With a few exceptions those who were members of the CCP Central Committee survived his purges, even after working against his policies. Mao preferred to exercise power not by chopping off heads, but by winning psychological triumphs over his rivals and compelling them to confess error.

When some of his policies sagged in failure, he sometimes publicly admitted his own blame. To Mao the hateful sin was not to fall into error, but to deny it and persist in it.

Far from being the steel automaton he was often made out to be, in advanced age Mao definitely felt the weight of his stormy years. His weariness was suggested in his seventies by one line of a poem he wrote: "Had heaven feelings, it would long since have grown old!" In his declining years Mao became, like Stalin, a somewhat paranoiac, oversuspicious recluse who worked alone at night, brooding over how far short his leaders and his people were falling in the goals he set for them.

Most of China's millions of peasants still persisted in the ancient practice of ancestor worship. Despite all his purges, it was also still necessary for Mao to keep an estimated fifty million Chinese with "bad class origins" under surveillance. Moreover, there were now literally millions of teenagers who, bored with the Thoughts of Chairman Mao, were bordering on juvenile delinquency in search of the excitement they had briefly enjoyed during their reign as Red Guards.

Mao refused to concede that the long era during which his ideas and methods dovetailed with China's needs might possibly have come to an end; that his country in the seventies might be a different world than the China of the forties, fifties, and sixties. With the development of its industrial economy, however, China was becoming urbanized. Its cities inevitably reflected western influence, with westernized schools, banks, transportation, and communication. Mao watched this development anxiously, fearful that westernization might also bring in its wake a revival of capitalism.

To strengthen China as a classless society, he had sought to wipe out differences between town and country, mental and manual work, the educated and uneducated. His campaigns to equalize all classes had been resisted and thwarted by China's educated class, however, arousing his ire against them.

Decades after victory, Mao felt a driving need to keep the spirit of revolution ablaze. "The revolution is also a feeling," he explained. "If we decide to make of it what the Russians are now doing—a feeling of the past—everything will fall apart. Our revolution cannot simply be the stabilization of a victory." That, he believed, would cause it to degenerate into a bureaucratic "capitalist restoration."

"What Mao has set himself to achieve," observed the London Economist in 1967, "is perpetual revolution—to be precise, a regular succession of upheavals, following each other at intervals of a generation or less. He believes that nothing short of this will keep the original revolutionary impetus alive." If some few hundred thousand Chinese officials had to be discarded in these upheavals, they seemed to Mao a small price to pay for assuring himself of hundreds of millions of revolutionary heirs and successors.

Now, though, at the end of his life, he was forced to recognize that he would die before he could complete the transformation of China. "For men of vision," he wrote in one poem, "we must seek among the present generation." He hoped that Chinese youth, like youth in many other parts of the world, would flock to the banner of the revolution and lift it from his aging hands.

Ironically, where his direct encouragement to revolutionary movements abroad had failed to bear fruit, his personal example won him unexpected converts among world youth. Raul Prebisch, Argentine economist at the United Nations, explained the fascination that Maoism held for Latin American youth:

> China is something the youth sees as an historical experiment to change the nature of men, to establish new forms of human coexistence. . . . There is admiration for a backward country that has been able to build an atomic bomb. And the figure of Mao—Mao is a charismatic figure. . . . The mere idea of a chaotic situation is attractive to the youth because they see Mao as trying to destroy the remnants of the old society. . . . They admire it as a way of clearing the ground for better things to come.

Mao encouraged world youth to denounce American intervention in Southeast Asia. He scoffed at Washington's insistence that if United States forces were withdrawn, all Vietnam would be overrun. Overrun, Mao demanded, by whom? By the Vietcong or North Vietnamese—all of whom were Vietnamese citizens? He acidly reminded Washington that it had also objected to China's being "overrun" by Chinese, because they were Red Chinese. What foreign troops were outside their own borders in Asian lands except the highly conspicuous Americans?

While Mao remained convinced of the inevitability of world revolution someday, he made it clear that China's armies would not be sent beyond her borders to fight; that they would only fight, in fact, if attacked by the United States or Russia. Those who sent troops beyond their own borders, he insisted, were the real culprits, who covered their own aggressions by raising a smoke screen about the "Chinese threat to world peace."

Mao reminded one journalist that in the days of the Manchu dynasty America had even then followed an imperialistic policy in the Pacific, calling it Manifest Destiny and alarming the American people about the "yellow peril" to frighten them into supporting it.

American attempts to crush people's wars around the world were doomed to failure, Mao believed, because the United States had been exposed as a "paper tiger." The people of China, Cuba, and North Vietnam had defied American power and won. Nuclear weapons would never frighten a determined people armed with rifles and revolutionary leadership.

"Experience in the class struggle in the era of imperialism," he declared, "teaches us that it is only by the power of the gun that the working class and the peasant masses can defeat the armed bourgeoisie and landlords. In this sense we may say that only with guns can the whole world be transformed."

In 1964 he had told French journalist Jules Roy, "Thirteen hundred years ago, under the T'ang dynasty, China . . . had one hundred sixty million inhabitants, and after ten years of war she was reduced to forty million. Bah! She recovered. . . . And the American millionaires are more concerned for their lives than we are . . . I do not think that they will dare bring on a war."

Mao continued to believe that his successful guerrilla tactics in fighting Chiang Kai-shek were a valid strategy for winning wars, if necessary, against great powers thirty years later. He enjoyed the power of his military feints to make the United States rush its forces this way and that, in alarm over Mao's intentions. If war did come, Mao did not expect to defeat the United States militarily but to bog it down hopelessly and weary it into withdrawal, as Ho Chi Minh had done.

Much of the West's confusion over Mao's policies was the result of a failure to appreciate some subtleties of Red Chinese diplomacy. Americans often became upset by Peking oratory, failing to distinguish between face-saving bravado, or propaganda for home consumption, and serious purpose.

Ironically, it was Nixon's Attorney General, pragmatic John Mitchell, who most closely approximated the Chinese technique when he defended the Nixon administration by telling reporters, "Watch what we do—not what we say!" Mao could not have agreed more.

Mao's most belligerent statements did not reflect, as they were often interpreted in the West, an eager desire for war. He greatly feared a U.S.–U.S.S.R. military alliance against China. His bluster was often intended to cloak that dread, as well as warn his people against being caught off guard. His chief weapon against the United States was the threat of world revolution, and he sought to worry Washington by sparking it.

The real power struggles from Mao's point of view were with Washington over whether Asia should be China's or America's sphere of influence, and with Moscow over leadership in the Communist world. Mao often appealed over the heads of both governments to the American and Russian people, urging them to repudiate their leaders' "imperialist" policies.

"The Chinese people know that United States imperialism has done many bad things to China and to the whole world as well," Mao declared. "They understand that only the United States ruling group is bad, while the people of the United States are very good." His Ping-Pong diplomacy of 1971 had been a people-to-people approach aimed at winning over popular opinion in the United States.

Mao often overestimated the power of American dissent against government policy, especially during the Vietnam War. In the spring of 1965 he had expressed confidence that the "toiling masses" would march on Washington, overthrow the "Wall Street government," and replace it with one friendly to Red China. He was baffled when even the most enormous antiwar demonstrations failed to bring about this development.

For all his brilliance in shaping the destiny of China, Mao remained essentially provincial, ill-equipped to understand the realities of the outside world except through the books he read, many of them by ninteenth-century authors. He neither spoke nor read any foreign language. He had made only two trips abroad, both brief and both to the city of Moscow. Cut off from the world by America's boycott as well as by his own isolation of China, Mao was not unlike the ancient Chinese emperors who, convinced that China was the center of civilization, had built the Great Wall to prevent contamination of Chinese society by the barbarian world.

Mao's position required him to be too tough, too remote, to be loved with warm affection by the Chinese masses, as Chu Teh was loved. Most Chinese, though, regarded him with awe and respect as an almost godlike figure who had liberated them from landlords, warlords, and imperialists, freed them from the terrible famines that had plagued China for centuries, wiped out illiteracy, brought new health standards to the countryside, ended official corruption, and inspired the Chinese people with a new sense of pride and purpose. Despite his mistakes and excesses and however harsh his methods, they continue to revere him as —in Lin Piao's words—"China's greatest liberator, statesman, teacher, strategist, philosopher, poet laureate and national hero."

Mao, in turn, counted on their support to sustain him in his race against death to secure his revolution for the centuries. At parades and celebrations in which two slogans on placards and banners were endlessly repeated he remained impassive as he viewed those expressing the wish "MAY CHAIRMAN MAO LIVE A VERY LONG TIME!" but he applauded, eyes glowing, when others passed by with the message closest to his heart: "MAY THE REVOLUTIONARY REGIME STAY RED FOR TEN THOUSAND GENERATIONS!"

"I am alone with the masses," he told André Malraux with quiet confidence. "Waiting."

China's destiny, when Mao is no longer here to guide it, remains a vast question mark. "Today the Chinese are afraid of one thing—that Mao will die," observed French journalist Maurice Ciantar. "They say that if he were to die tomorrow, China would be plunged into a bloodbath."

"It's possible," agreed French diplomat Jacques Guillermaz, "for he's the one who holds the whole system together."

Whether on balance Mao Tse-tung will be remembered as a good or an evil man, or a unique combination of both, will inevitably depend on the political glasses through which he is viewed. Both within and without China he had millions of admirers and enemies, as well as millions who had ambivalent feelings about him.

Most would agree, however, that Mao was a historically important figure who set in motion forces that not only changed Chinese society but also affected the balance of world power, perhaps forever. He certainly left an indelible imprint upon his country and his people for generations to come.

The revolutionary China he built is likely to endure as a huge Asian pyramid to his memory. Whether, however, it will remain the same Red China that Mao Tse-tung created, shaped, and loved, only our own descendants will be able to know for sure.

# Bibliography

*(\* Indicates recommended reading.)*

Canning, John, ed. *100 Great Kings, Queens and Rulers of the World.* New York: Taplinger Publishing Company, 1967.

Carr, Albert Z. *Truman, Stalin and Peace.* Garden City, N.Y.: Doubleday & Company, Inc., 1950.

\* Chen Chang-feng. *On the Long March with Chairman Mao.* Peking: Foreign Language Press, 1959.

\* Ch'ên, Jerome. *Mao and the Chinese Revolution.* New York: Oxford University Press, 1965.

De Toledano, Ralph. *Spies, Dupes and Diplomats.* New Rochelle, N.Y.: Arlington House, 1967.

Del Vayo, Julio Alvarez. *China Triumphs.* New York: Monthly Review Press, 1964.

Donnelly, Desmond. *Struggle for the World.* New York: St. Martin's Press, 1965.

Draskovich, Slobodan M. *Tito, Moscow's Trojan Horse.* Chicago: Henry Regnery Company, 1957.

Fairbank, John King. *The United States and China.* Cambridge, Mass.: Harvard University Press, 1948.

\* Floyd, David. *Mao Against Khrushchev.* New York and London: Frederick A. Praeger, 1963.

\* Forman, Harrison. *Report from Red China.* New York: Henry Holt and Company, 1945.

Griffith, Brigadier General Samuel B. *Peking and People's*

*Wars.* New York, Washington, D.C., and London: Frederick A. Praeger, 1966.

Gunther, John. *Inside Asia.* New York and London: Harper & Brothers, 1939.

———. *Inside Russia Today.* New York: Harper & Brothers, 1957.

———. *The Riddle of MacArthur.* New York: Harper & Brothers, 1950.

Hayter, Sir William. *The Kremlin and the Embassy.* New York: The Macmillan Company, 1966.

House Un-American Activities Committee. *Guerrilla Warfare Advocates in the United States.* Washington, D.C.: U.S. Government Printing Office, 1968.

Hu, C. T. *The Education of National Minorities in Communist China.* Washington, D.C.: U.S. Department of Health, Education, and Welfare, Office of Education, 1970.

Kai-yu Hsu. *Chou En-lai: China's Gray Eminence.* Garden City, N.Y.: Doubleday & Company, Inc., 1968.

Lacouture, Jean. *Ho Chi Minh.* New York: Random House, 1968.

* Lifton, Robert Jay, ed. *America and the Asian Revolutions.* Aldine Publishing Company, 1970.

Lindqvist, Sven. *China in Crisis.* New York: Thomas Y. Crowell Company, 1963.

Malraux, André. *Anti-Memoirs.* New York, Chicago, and San Francisco: Holt, Rinehart and Winston, 1968.

* Mao Tse-tung. *An Anthology of His Writings.* New York, Ontario, and London: New American Library, 1962.

* Payne, Robert. *Chinese Diaries 1941–1946.* New York: Weybright and Talley, 1970.

Pethybridge, R. W. *A History of Postwar Russia.* New York: New American Library, Inc., 1966.

* Roy, Jules. *Journey through China.* London: Faber and Faber Limited, 1965.

* Schram, Stuart. *Mao Tse-tung.* Baltimore: Penguin Books, 1967.

* Schurmann, Franz, and Schell, Orville, eds. *Communist China.* New York: Random House, 1967.

* Siao, Emi. *Mao Tse-tung: His Childhood and Youth.* Bombay: The People's Publishing House, 1953.

* Simone, Vera. *China in Revolution.* Greenwich, Conn.: Fawcett Publications, Inc., 1968.

* Smedley, Agnes. *The Great Road.* New York: Monthly Review Press, 1956.

* Snow, Edgar. *Red Star over China.* New York: Grove Press, Inc., 1968.

Spector, Ivar. *The First Russian Revolution: Its Impact on Asia.* Englewood Cliffs, N.J.: Prentice-Hall, Inc., 1962.

* Stilwell, Joseph W. *The Stilwell Papers.* New York: Macfadden-Bartell Corporation, 1962.

Sulzberger, C. L. *A Long Row of Candles.* New York and Toronto: The Macmillan Company, 1969.

Topolski, Felix. *Holy China.* Boston: Houghton Mifflin Company, 1968.

Trager, Frank N., ed. *Mao: War or Peace?* American-Asian Educational Exchange, Inc., 1970.

Tung Chi-ping and Evans, Humphrey. *The Thought Revolution.* New York: Coward-McCann, Inc., 1966.

* White, Theodore H. *China: The Roots of Madness.* New York: W. W. Norton & Company, Inc., 1968.

Wint, Guy. *Spotlight on Asia.* Baltimore: Penguin Books, 1959.

Wise, David, and Ross, Thomas B. *The Espionage Establishment.* New York: Random House, 1967.

Wolfe, Bertram D. *Communist Totalitarianism.* Boston: Beacon Press, 1956.

Yutang, Lin. *The Secret Name.* London, Melbourne, and Toronto: William Heinemann, Ltd., 1959.

Also consulted were issues of *The Center Magazine, Foreign Affairs, Horizon, Fortune, Free China Weekly, Life, Look, Mankind, Man's Magazine, Marriage and Family Living, The Na-*

*tion, The New Republic, Newsweek, The New York Times Magazine, Orbis, The Reporter, The Saturday Evening Post, Time, U.S. News and World Report,* and *Vital Speeches,* as well as special material obtained from the Chinese (Formosan) Information Service and the Novosti (Soviet) Press Agency.

# Index